THE PROPHETS ON MAIN STREET

The Prophets on Main Street

J. ELLIOTT CORBETT

JOHN KNOX PRESS

RICHMOND, VIRGINIA

Scripture quotations are from the Revised Standard Version, copyright 1946 and 1952 by the Division of Christian Education of the National Council of the Churches of Christ in the United States of America.

The paraphrase of Amos has been revised from "Amos Today" which appeared in *The Pulpit*, July, 1956.

Fourth printing 1966

LIBRARY OF CONGRESS CATALOG CARD NUMBER: 65-10428

© M. E. BRATCHER 1965

PRINTED IN THE UNITED STATES OF AMERICA

J. 3778 (WB) D. 38

TO MY MOTHER

Clara Helen Swanson

CONTENTS

INTRODUCTION

The Old Testament prophets were not crystal-ball gazers. When they prophesied under the inspiration of God, they spoke most frequently about the appalling social conditions of their day. They were not foretellers; they were forth-tellers. It was not their mission to forecast events but to speak on behalf of God in the context of their times. This does not mean that the prophets were unconcerned about the future. They predicted prosperity or devastation, peace or war, depending upon the degree of moral responsibility of king and people before God.

Lonely men, the prophets were often religious leaders without followers, although sometimes they had a few disciples. In the countryside, on the hilltop, or out in the desert, they especially felt the presence of God. But it was when witnessing to the flagrant violation of God's will in the cities that they could not contain themselves. Like Jeremiah, they were "weary with holding it in" (Jer. 20:9). Or, like Second Isaiah, they attested, "He made my mouth like a sharp sword" (Isa. 49:2).

It is difficult for us to understand the anguish in the hearts of the prophets. Because they were very close to the people, when it was necessary for them to pronounce judgment they took no sadistic pleasure in it. Rather, they must have winced under the lash of their own tongues and cringed under the hammer blows of their own words. Often they begged God to stay his anger.

Their purpose as instruments of God was to redeem rather than to proclaim judgment. They wanted their people to turn from sin rather than reap the consequences of their disobedience. They brooded over the people and wept over resistant spirits, much as Jesus wept over Jerusalem for its rejection of his teachings.

The prophets were often despised, sometimes feared, but always respected. What they had said proved upon the reflection of later generations to be true. In bane and blessing their prophecies were fulfilled.

What has been attempted in the paraphrases of this volume is not to rewrite the Scriptures, but to make the prophetic material more meaningful to our contemporary society. The accomplishment of a similar objective is the aim of every sermon. It is hoped that readers of this book will be moved to return to the prophets and ponder their deeper meanings for our own times.

I have made no attempt to "Phillippize" the Old Testament. Only J. B. Phillips in his inimitable way can summon the appropriate language for this task. In the process of paraphrasing five prophetic books, the question uppermost in my mind has been, "What would the prophets, given their spirit, be inclined to say about this matter today?" The theological position of the prophets has been generally preserved, but I have attributed to them some further spiritual insights as a result of the twenty-five centuries of human experience that have intervened. For this reason the theology may be less judgmental and will depend more upon the impartial operation of divine law than upon direct intervention by an aroused deity.

Four of the paraphrases are in free verse while Jonah is written in satirical narrative. In other words, the paraphrases are framed in the form in which they were originally cast. All of the paraphrases deal with current religious, social, and political problems, with an emphasis upon international affairs. I have attempted to preserve the spirit and passion of the prophets as they would view today's scene, but I have avoided sticking slavishly to the original text.

For the observant reader there will be obvious omissions. These are not studied omissions; they exist only because the passages did not strike fire at the time of writing. Subject matter has also been included which has no close counterpart in the original prophets, including such subjects as Communism, race, and the Peace Corps. These, however, represent the kind of significant topics the ever alert prophets would be apt to consider today.

It was not originally planned to include a treatment of the "suffering servant" theme. To deal with this poem would be tantamount to an ancient Hebrew touching the Ark of the Covenant, so it seemed. However, as the tempo of the non-violent direct action movement for racial freedom quickened, the theme appeared too timely to omit.

Admittedly the transition points between paraphrases are not always smooth. Perhaps it is in this respect that I have been most true to the prophets! Also in the writings of the Old Testament it is not always clear when a prophet speaks in his own name and when he is speaking an oracle of the Lord. I do not presume in these paraphrases to claim that anything that is written is on the "oracle" level. I can only hope that it is not contrary to the will of God.

I would like to emphasize that the contemporary paraphrases as framed in this volume are not conceived to be the last word— or even the next to the last word. Rather, it is hoped that each reader will be encouraged to go back to the Bible and try his own hand at the adaptation of the message of the prophets to the rapidly changing modern scene.

Where Scripture material is used directly in the paraphrased sections, it appears in the text in italics. Biblical references for the paraphrases are indicated with the titles and in parentheses, should the reader wish to consult the source in its original context. The Revised Standard Version of the Bible has been used throughout.

Some readers already thoroughly familiar with the life and times of the prophets may wish to turn directly to the paraphrases themselves. Most readers will find it advantageous to read the brief commentaries for each book of prophecy and to familiarize themselves with the selections of scriptural material preceding the paraphrases.

I wish to record a note of appreciation to those who have read the paraphrases and who have made helpful suggestions: Dr. Lowell B. Hazzard, The Reverend J. Emery Fleming, and my colleague, The Reverend W. Rodney Shaw. They, of course, are not responsible for the shortcomings that I am sure exist in this volume.

I feel greatly indebted to my Old Testament professor, Dr. James B. Pritchard, who first stirred my excitement over the prophets. Last, but most important of all, thanks to my wife who originally suggested that I attempt to place the prophets on Main Street.

I | AMOS

Amos—His Times and Ours

Amos was a layman. Unlike many of the other prophetic figures, he had no formal education. He had received no special training in either his religious heritage or literary technique. Although a citizen of the southern kingdom of Judah, he proclaimed his message in the streets of the northern kingdom of Israel. Though branded as an "outside agitator" by the religious leaders of Israel, the people listened to his message and he succeeded in "getting under their skin."

The home of Amos was in the wilderness of Tekoa, a bleak area of limestone hills about six miles south of Jerusalem. Meager vegetation provided scant pasturage for Amos' small flock of sheep. He barely mustered a living by laboring also as a dresser of sycamore (fig) trees, the pricking of whose fruit encouraged ripening. Seeking a market for his products in the larger trading centers of Israel, Amos traveled to the cities of Bethel, Gilgal, Samaria, and even Damascus.

The luxurious living he observed in these cities appalled and deeply troubled him. The lack of concern by the well-to-do for the oppressed and unfortunate aroused his anger. Amos was moved to speak out bluntly and forthrightly in the name of God against injustice.

The lowly shepherd of Tekoa may have seemed ill-equipped to issue divine pronouncements in cities where prophets were trained in fluency of speech and where many of his hearers were far better educated than he. But Amos had an educated heart, and under the compelling power of the Spirit of God he spoke some of the most striking, terse, direct, and passionately poetic lines to be found in all the Bible.

THE KINGDOM OF ISRAEL UNDER JEROBOAM II

The ministry of Amos occurred during the long reign of Jeroboam II (786-746 B.C.). It was a time of great prosperity and substantial security for the northern kingdom of Israel. During the early years of Jeroboam's reign, Assyria had defeated Syria, but was in such need of recovery from that blood-letting struggle that Israel was left relatively free. Under Jeroboam II, Israel reached the height of its territorial expansion. Trade flowed along the routes running through many cities of Israel. The upper classes owned both winter houses and summer houses and decorated them with ivory. The people felt that such good times were strong evidence of Yahweh's favor. They reciprocated in turn by offering their choicest animals for sacrifice and by participating in religious celebrations with at least outward loyalty.

Yet all was not well in Israel. Under the influence of the Canaanite fertility cults, sacred prostitution had become commonplace. Religious festivals degenerated into occasions for gluttony and drunkenness. Merchants, in order to make a high profit, sold wheat mixed with chaff. The poor, so completely at the mercy of the wealthy classes, were often sold into slavery to pay for their debts.

What disturbed Amos most was the silence of the prophets. Instead of raising their voices in protest they often descended to the level of debauchery themselves. "You made the Nazirites drink wine," cried Amos, "and commanded the prophets, saying, 'You shall not prophesy'" (2:12). Amos could contain himself no longer.

THE MAJOR TEACHINGS OF AMOS

One of the major truths Amos sought to communicate to the people of Samaria was that *God rules over and judges all nations.* As the prophet denounces the transgressions of their neighbors—Damascus, Gaza, Tyre, Edom, Ammon, Moab, and even Judah—one can almost visualize the Israelites smiling smugly and nodding their heads. If Amos had only stopped there, he could have retained his popularity as the ancient counterpart of a modern Soviet demonologist. But instead he went on to devastatingly describe the moral failure of the Israelites themselves, which equally deserved terrifying judgment.

It was not as though the Israelites had not had abundant opportunity to repent. Frequently they had been chastened by the Lord—through famine, drought, blight, and pestilence, yet despite all this, said the spokesman for God, "you did not return to me" (4:6-11). Because you went your own way, ignoring all warnings, there is nothing left for you now except to "prepare to meet your God" (4:12).

Amos saw the people under a double judgment. They not only knew better, but they were living under the covenant which God had made with them when he delivered them from Egypt. They were therefore expected to be more responsible and disciplined, yet they had betrayed the Almighty. Many Israelites felt that when the day of the Lord came, it would be a day of triumph and rejoicing, a day when God would bestow his special benefits upon them. But Amos corrected this misconception. Because of their behavior, the day of the Lord would be for them a day of darkest gloom with no brightness in it.

Still another principle which Amos preached to Israel was that *Yahweh demanded righteousness above religiosity*. When the people came on three-day pilgrimages to Bethel and Gilgal, purportedly to bring their sacrifices, tithes, and freewill offerings, they spent much of their time in gross wickedness (4:4, 5). Ritual replaced righteousness and became a mere cover-up for transgression. Pilgrimages to the shrines of the unholy cities were blatant hypocrisy.

Amos proclaimed that the Lord despised their "solemn assemblies" and their religious feasts which had become occasions for gluttony. Burnt offerings, cereal offerings, and peace offerings are no substitute for a penitent heart. What God truly desires is that "justice roll down like waters, and righteousness like an everlasting stream."

A primary strain running throughout the book of Amos is that *the Lord condemns social sin*. Personal corruption had become so embedded in the customs of society that many licentious practices were accepted by the community without a second thought. "It must be all right," the people said, "everybody does it." Amos was unmistakably blunt in speaking about the injustices of society which he felt broke the heart of God. He was especially displeased with the wealthy landowner class who "trampled upon the poor." Apparently they kept their farm laborers in a quasi-indentured servant status, requiring such a large share of the wheat harvest that the workers were always in debt. Amos objected to the rich building both summer and winter houses for themselves when so many of the poor had not so much as a shelter for over their heads.

Amos pronounced his woes against the ostentatious leisure class who amused themselves in bored sophistication, but were not "grieved over the ruin of Joseph." These irresponsible "opulent beatniks" neither knew nor cared that Israel was on the brink of destruction. The idle rich women, unconcerned over the lot of the poor, were scorned by Amos as "cows of Bashan." He minced no words in warning the eighth-century counterpart of the female cocktail set of the disaster impending for the corrupt capital city of Samaria. Like the carcasses of dead animals, he predicted, their corpses would be removed from the ruined city (Samaria was sacked by the Assyrians not many years later, 722-721 B.C.).

Nor did the politicians escape the observing eye of Amos. They were willing to "take a bribe" even if it meant forsaking the interests of their decent constituents. The merchants were also condemned who in their greed could not wait for the Sabbath to pass so they could get back to their unscrupulous business practices. Like the dishonest butcher who puts his hand on the scale, the wheat merchants dealt "deceitfully with false balances." They made the measure small and the price great. Fraudulent profits were in turn used to compound evil—to buy the poverty-stricken as slaves for a few silver coins, and "the needy for a pair of sandals."

Against the backdrop of these injustices, Amos reveals his vision of the Lord with a plumb line in his hand. He is setting the plumb line in the midst of the house of Jacob, a house with sagging walls, about to collapse.

In chapter nine Amos describes the attempts of the desperate Israelites to escape destruction. He warns those who comfort themselves that they will get away safely if disaster should come. Whether they dig into Sheol, climb up to heaven, hide on a mountain or at the bottom of the sea, the Lord who commands the heavens and the earth will find them and bring them under judgment.

We need to remember that in spite of Amos' dire predictions of doom, his purpose was not to terrify the people or to glory in their punishment. He preached that they might repent. "Seek the Lord and live." Had the people turned from their sins, no one in Israel would have offered more joyous prayers of thanksgiving than Amos.

What was the reaction of Israel to the bold pronouncements of the shepherd of Tekoa? The priest of Bethel, Amaziah, reported Amos to King Jeroboam as guilty of conspiracy. The complaint of the priest was not that Amos uttered untruth, but that "the land is not able to bear all his words" (7:10). He suggested that Amos go home to Judah where he belonged. "Prophesy there; but never again prophesy at Bethel" (7:12-13). In other words, your prophesies are an embarrassment to the elite here, for "it is the king's sanctuary" (7:13).

We do not know what happened to Amos, whether he was stoned to death or whether he went back to his home in Judah. But whatever happened, his appraisal of eighth-century Israel was so correct and his judgment so far-sighted that later generations preserved his prophetic witness. His words stand today to judge another generation.

AMOS' MESSAGE FOR THE MODERN ERA

Several general principles proclaimed by Amos are particularly pertinent to our own nation today. One of these, restated, is: *The United States must expect to be judged by God and his moral law on the basis of its own behavior.* Although we have been blessed by God as a nation, no more than Israel can we expect to receive preferred status. For God, as Amos declared, is the Judge of *all* nations. Too often we have adopted the double standard of judging the Soviets either by their unseemly actions or by the damning words of some long-dead Communist prophet, and judging ourselves by our good intentions and the idealism of the Declaration of Independence.

Some examples of how reluctant we are to judge our own nation objectively, as God must judge us, include the following:

1. It was only when Soviet missile bases were discovered on Cuban soil that many Americans for the first time were able to grasp the fear felt by the Russian people because of our advance missile bases in places like Turkey, directly on the border of the Soviet Union. Now, of course, our Jupiter missiles, old-fashioned and good only for first-strike, have been removed from Turkey and Italy.

2. Americans profess the ideals of freedom of the press and freedom of speech. We attempt to crack the Iron Curtain by flooding Eastern Europe with American magazines, books, films, and Voice of America and Radio Free Europe broadcasts, all in an effort to spread the truth. Yet we seem to be fearful of the truth about Communist regimes penetrating the United States. Thus we severely limit travel visas for our citizens to Cuba and we prohibit them to Communist China. We make it difficult for our newsmen to get into Cuba and impossible for them to get into China. How then are *we* to know the truth?

3. In 1946 the U. S. Senate adopted the Connally Amendment. This reservation was attached to our acceptance of the compulsory jurisdiction of the International Court of Justice. This "self-judging clause" means that we reserve the right to determine in advance whether or not a case in which we are involved ought to be submitted to the World Court. It thus appears to other nations that we wish to remain a law unto ourselves rather than being willing to risk a possible adverse decision by submitting all justiciable cases to this international body.

4. When American arms help to implement military coups in such places as the Dominican Republic and Honduras, surely then our use of military assistance to "strengthen the free world" needs to be brought into question.

We ought to be cognizant of another contemporary application of Amos' teaching: *The church cannot allow ritual, financial affairs, building programs, or other secondary matters to interfere with the implementation of righteousness.* Elaborate forms of worship, mass rallies, suppers, new organs, or large collections sometimes seem to be the most important matters in the life of a church. Then we read Amos again and discover that God desires justice and righteousness more than feasts, solemn assemblies, ritual, offerings, and fine music (5:21-24).

We may believe that if we remodel the sanctuary, install a communion rail, secure new altar cloths, and bedeck the minister in colorful vestments, something significant has been achieved for the Kingdom. Actually in such a priestly environment the preacher may feel it inappropriate to utter the prophetic messages the people most need to hear.

When we deplore the plight of the Russian Orthodox Church today under the restrictions imposed by a Communist government, we should recall that this same church before the 1917 revolution found its major expression in liturgical worship and elaborate ritual. The church then showed little compassion for the serfs, nor did it speak out against cruel practices of government officials or the luxury-loving aristocracy. Instead most of the priests were concerned with gold-leafing their church domes and so bejewelling their lectern Bibles that it required extreme effort to open the Book to read such prophets as Amos!

Christians who would heed Amos' message must always be seeking ways to establish justice in their communities, in the courts, in business, in political and social life. They will strive to improve race relations, to meet welfare needs adequately, to promote mental health, to provide good schools and recreational outlets. As St. Paul admonished the Christians in Rome: "Offer your bodies in a *living* sacrifice . . . that is your rational worship" (Rom. 12:1, Goodspeed, italics mine).

Amos' message might be applied in still another way to contemporary times: *Christians must be concerned about sin in society as well as about personal morality.* To be a bank embezzler or a wife-slayer is to be considered sinful by the majority of people. But if a shrewd businessman organizes a combine of corporations in such a way as to enrich the board of directors without paying dividends to the stockholders, he may be thought of as a financial wizard. Or in wartime, if a plane bombs the enemy nation, killing thousands of innocent citizens, both the pilot and the bombardier may be rewarded for heroism. As Dr. Reinhold Niebuhr said years ago: "There is an increasing tendency among modern men to imagine themselves ethical because they have delegated their vices to larger and larger groups."[1]

Alcoholism is a personal problem for some five million individuals in our nation, yet it is closely related to such social problems as crime, delinquency, poverty, and automobile accidents. For example, research by the National Safety Council indicates that "frequently 50% or more of the fatal accidents have involved drinking drivers or drinking pedestrians."[2] In the rather typical year of 1960 there were 38,200 deaths due to motor vehicle accidents. Fifty percent of this number (related to alcohol) would be 19,100. In the tragic three-year Korean War, there were a total of 33,629 Americans killed. Thus, one can easily see that in three years on the highway there are more alcohol-related deaths than there were American fatalities during the entire Korean conflict. Yet we Americans do not become righteously indignant, but continue to tolerate a profusion of roadside drinking places, primarily accessible by automobile.

Residential segregation is perhaps the greatest social sin in the United States today. A recent study of church members in a white suburban area of Los Angeles indicated that more than one-half of the Christians polled would disapprove of a Negro family of similar education and income moving into their neighborhood. Integrating of schools and of church congregations can be expected to be no more than token so long as residential segregation is a continuing policy. As Dr. Roger Ragan states: "Perhaps local churches have talked too much about getting their own houses in order to the neglect of community conditions which make it next to impossible for them to be inclusive."[3]

If Amos were living today he would surely be concerned about the predicament of the chronically poor: the illiterate, unskilled outcasts of our affluent nation. He would be indignant at the comfortable middle-class citizens and the tax-conscious politicians who rejoice in slashing the relief rolls. He might urge them instead to invest enough resources in rehabilitation so that such families could become self-respecting contributors to society, instead of perpetuating poverty from generation to generation.

Undoubtedly the shepherd from Tekoa would challenge many of our accepted social practices. He might probe into situations that others considered none of his business. Yet the prophet Amos would not easily be silenced by those who denounced him as a "meddling outside agitator."

Selections from Amos

DOOM FOR NEARBY NATIONS   1:6-7, 11; 2:4-5

Thus says the LORD:
   "For three transgressions of Gaza,
     and for four, I will not revoke the punishment;
   because they carried into exile a whole people
     to deliver them up to Edom.
   So I will send a fire upon the wall of Gaza,
     and it shall devour her strongholds. . . . "
Thus says the LORD:
   "For three transgressions of Edom,
     and for four, I will not revoke the punishment;
   because he pursued his brother with the sword,
     and cast off all pity . . . "
Thus says the LORD:
   "For three transgressions of Judah,
     and for four, I will not revoke the punishment;
   because they have rejected the law of the LORD,
     and have not kept his statutes,
   but their lies have led them astray,
     after which their fathers walked.
   So I will send a fire upon Judah,
     and it shall devour the strongholds of Jerusalem."

THE SIN AND DOWNFALL OF ISRAEL   2:6-7

Thus says the LORD:
   "For three transgressions of Israel,
     and for four, I will not revoke the punishment;
   because they sell the righteous for silver,
     and the needy for a pair of shoes—
   they that trample the head of the poor into the dust of the
       earth,
     and turn aside the way of the afflicted . . . "

THE PLIGHT OF THE WICKED WOMEN 4:1-3

"Hear this word, you cows of Bashan,
    who are in the mountain of Samaria,
who oppress the poor, who crush the needy,
    who say to their husbands, 'Bring, that we may drink!'
The Lord God has sworn by his holiness
    that, behold, the days are coming upon you,
when they shall take you away with hooks,
    even the last of you with fishhooks.
And you shall go out through the breaches,
    every one straight before her;
    and you shall be cast forth into Harmon,*"

                    says the LORD.

WHAT GOD DESIRES 5:21-24

I hate, I despise your feasts,
    and I take no delight in your solemn assemblies.
Even though you offer me your burnt offerings and cereal
        offerings,
    I will not accept them,
and the peace offerings of your fatted beasts
    I will not look upon.
Take away from me the noise of your songs;
    to the melody of your harps I will not listen.
But let justice roll down like waters,
    and righteousness like an ever-flowing stream.

THE PROPHET'S CALL 7:14-15

Then Amos answered Amaziah, "I am no prophet, nor a prophet's son; but I am a herdsman, and a dresser of sycamore trees, and the LORD took me from following the flock, and the LORD said to me, 'Go, prophesy to my people Israel.' "

THE GREEDY MERCHANTS 8:4-6

Hear this, you who trample upon the needy,
    and bring the poor of the land to an end,

* The refuse pile.

saying, "When will the new moon be over,
 that we may sell grain?
And the sabbath,
 that we may offer wheat for sale,
that we may make the ephah small and the shekel great,
 and deal deceitfully with false balances,
that we may buy the poor for silver
 and the needy for a pair of sandals,
 and sell the refuse of the wheat?"

THE RESTORATION OF ISRAEL 9:13-15

"Behold, the days are coming," says the LORD,
 "When the plowman shall overtake the reaper
 and the treader of grapes him who sows the seed;
the mountains shall drip sweet wine,
 and all the hills shall flow with it.
I will restore the fortunes of my people Israel,
 and they shall rebuild the ruined cities and inhabit
   them;
they shall plant vineyards and drink their wine,
 and they shall make gardens and eat their fruit.
I will plant them upon their land,
 and they shall never again be plucked up
 out of the land which I have given them,"

           says the LORD your God.

Amos—Prophet of Justice in an Atomic Age

ORACLE FOR TRANSGRESSORS   (1:3—2:8)

Thus says the Lord:
  For three transgressions of Germany, and for four,
      I will not turn it back;
  for you have destroyed millions in your gas chambers,
      and persecuted my people without pity.
  Therefore a wall shall divide you,
      and foreign nations shall occupy you.
  For three transgressions of Japan, and for four,
      I will not turn it back,
  because you ravaged your neighbors,
      and oppressed the weak through conquest.
  So I will make of you an armed camp and a naval base,
      though in your constitution you outlaw war.
  For three transgressions of Russia, and for four,
      I will not turn it back,
  for you have kept your people in ignorance by censorship,
      and falsely convinced them of their prosperity.
  You have rattled your missiles above the noisy proclamations
      of your peaceful intentions,
      and tampered with the freedom of friendly nations.
  So I will tip your hand to your opponents,
      and saddle your people with the heavy burden of armaments.
  For three transgressions of America, and for four,
      I will not turn it back,
  because you have dropped atom bombs without remorse
      upon open cities,
      and stockpiled H-bombs ad infinitum.
  So I will make other nations fear your power and envy your
          wealth.
  Your doom is assured, your demise is at hand.

For I hear your songs of self-praise;
  I listen also to your criticism of others.
But though I remove the wax from my straining ears,
    I cannot hear your voice raised in self-judgment or
    repentance.
There is wailing in the streets of Washington,
  and confusion on the expressways of Chicago.
There is atomic dust over the city of Los Angeles;
  no smog lay as heavy or as long.
The cries of children in New York City
  are heard above the siren's scream.
For you trusted in the makers of atom bombs,
  but not in the Maker of the atom.

IDLE IRRESPONSIBILITY   (6:4-7)

Hear this word, you who while away the idle hours, saying,
  "When will the next bingo game be played?" or
  "What club shall we go to tonight?"
Woe unto you who go to deep freezers, saying,
  "Shall it be steak or chicken?"
  but care little for my children in India who have no rice.
For I will take away what you think you have,
  and give it to those who have none.

THE VENEER OF PIETY   (5:21-24)

I hate your new church buildings,
  I take no great pleasure in your rising membership rolls.
The tinkle of your treasuries gives me an earache!
  Take away from my sight your veneer of piety.
To your boasts of being a Christian nation I will not listen.
But let justice roll down like waters,
  and righteousness like an ever-flowing stream.

A REFUGE FOR THE FEW

Woe unto you unless you search after *my* ways
  and follow after *my* commandments!

Your grandfathers found America a haven for the many,
  but you have made it a refuge for the few.
Your poetry at the gate says,
  "Give me your tired, your poor,
  your huddled masses yearning to be free."
But your law at the gate says,
  "Your nationality is wrong,
  your politics is wrong,
  your color is wrong,
  you were born in the wrong place—
  stay home!"

A SUPERIOR RACE

Give heed to my word, O Jackson!
Stop not your ears, O Cleveland!
Turn not away, Prince Edward County.
To prove that you are a superior race,
  you close down all your schools,
lest your white children suffer the indignity
  of sitting beside colored children in classroom proximity.
For you boast of your white supremacy,
  and flaunt the highest court in the land.
Surely your fall shall be certain,
  your pride laid to rest in the dust.

ALCOHOL + GASOLINE = BLOOD

Woe unto you, hypocrites! who tolerate TV beer commercials
  to sponsor your national sport,
yet you are puzzled when teen-agers turn for enjoyment
  from baseball to beer-drinking.
You clutter your highways with taverns,
  though when alcohol and gasoline are mixed,
  too often they turn to blood.
You piously proclaim, "What's the harm in a little drink?"
Yet you show only disgust at the skid-row plight
  of millions of dead-end alcoholics.

PRIVILEGE-SEEKERS

Your farmers want cushioning price supports,
    your businessmen seek cost-plus contracts;
your unions guaranteed annual wages,
    your veterans lobby for special privileges.
Yet a cry goes up from the same people:
    "Down with high prices! Down with inflation! Down with
      big government!"
Every pressure group among you wants cake—
    but let the other man pay for it.

THE RACE IN SPACE

Hear this word,
    you who shoot rockets out into space!
      Have you solved all problems on your earth?
Is it prestige you seek to buttress your unsure confidence?
    Do you expect to impress the third of the world that is
      uncommitted,
      those less-developed nations who are hungry, illiterate, and
        diseased?
Bend your ear, O America! Do not be deceived!
The space *they* care about
    is their empty stomachs;
the shots that will most impress *them*
    are penicillin shots!

CALL OF THE PROPHET (7:14-15)

I am not a called preacher who must depend for his security
    upon those who hire him;
who must please the people of the pews,
    but not necessarily the God of the heavens.
My calling is of God, for I am only a poor shepherd
    and the pruner of fruit trees.
But *the Lord took me from following the flock, and the Lord
said to me, "Go, prophesy to my people* of America."

II | FIRST ISAIAH

First Isaiah—His Times and Ours

THE LIFE AND TIMES OF ISAIAH

Isaiah, the eighth-century prophet of Jerusalem, differed from most other major prophetic figures in serving as a political advisor at the highest level—a confidant of kings. Well educated and undoubtedly steeped in religious training, he was of a nobleman's family and thus had access to the royal court. Of this special privilege he took utmost advantage. Highly respected, he seems to have held the king's ear even when he voiced unpopular opinions and counsel.

HISTORICAL BACKGROUND

The author of chapters 1-39 of Isaiah is often called First Isaiah so as to distinguish him from the writer of chapters 40-66 who lived in a later period. The public life of First Isaiah spanned some forty years of a most difficult period in Hebrew history. The dominant world power was Assyria to the northeast. Tiny Judah was alternately trapped and pushed by three forces —a desire for independence, the temptation to join alliances to enhance her security, and the constant threat of subjugation or assimilation by the powerful Assyrian kingdom. Invading armies periodically marched into Judah. Her immediate neighbor to the north, the kingdom of Israel, eventually disappeared with the siege and fall of Samaria.

The prophet Isaiah served in this environment as spokesman for God. Beginning his prophetic activity as a young man in the year of the death of King Uzziah, who ruled from 783 to 742 B.C., Isaiah continued his work during the reign of three other kings of Judah from 742 to 687 B.C.: Jotham, Ahaz, and Hezekiah.

The prophet received his call "in the year that King Uzziah died." Uzziah's successful reign had been marked by peace and prosperity. As far as the people were concerned it was not "time for a change." But change came, and with it great anxiety about the future. For during that very year, Tiglath-pileser III of As-syria invaded northern Israel and exacted a heavy tribute.

Sitting in the temple one day, brooding over the situation that confronted his unhappy land, Isaiah had a deep religious experi-ence (6:1-8). He was overwhelmed by a sense of the holiness of God—a holiness which by comparison made him feel like "a man of unclean lips" dwelling "in the midst of a people of unclean lips." Holiness in early Old Testament times had denoted largely the separateness and aloofness of God without any moral over-tones. Isaiah sees God's holiness in the fullness of its ethical rich-ness. It is in the presence of this kind of God that he senses his own unworthiness.

Then a voice from heaven speaks to his anxious soul, "Your guilt is taken away, and your sin forgiven." When the voice of the Lord says, "Who will go for us?" Isaiah becomes conscious of the great need of his people for redemption and for restored faith in a God who is himself holy and who expects holiness of his peo-ple. With such an awareness of the awesome task to which he is called, Isaiah accepts his commission as a prophet.

WHAT SORT OF MAN WAS ISAIAH?

Despite Isaiah's education, nobility, and ready access to the royal court, Judah's rulers were inclined more often than not to ignore his advice.

Although he might have had reason, by virtue of background, to remain aloof as part of the socially elite, he was primarily an aristocrat of the spirit. Equally at home with kings and com-moners, he spoke with the dignity and authority of one who knew he was under divine command.

Married and the father of two children, Isaiah was apparently a devoted family man. He referred to his wife as "the proph-etess" and gave his children names which witnessed to his own prophetic message.

THE MAJOR TEACHINGS OF ISAIAH

To Isaiah, insatiable greed, drunken debauchery, and indifference to the predicament of the poor reflected a serious condition —rejection of the will of God, whose character is basically ethical. Isaiah is deeply concerned that "the faithful city has become a harlot." He is appalled by the shallow vanity of the haughty young women of the day "mincing along as they go." He calls into question those whose primary concern in life is avariciously to "join house to house." The political leader who "loves a bribe and runs after gifts" comes under his lashing. Those who "rise early in the morning" to "run after strong drink" are denounced by Isaiah's fiery tongue.

Isaiah is nauseated by meaningless religious rites—burnt offerings, the multiplication of "new moons" and "appointed feasts," the spreading forth of hands, and the mouthing of long prayers. Instead the Lord God wants goodness, justice, relief for the oppressed, and compassion for the helpless and distressed.

THE PROPHET AS POLITICAL COUNSELOR

Since Isaiah found that relatively few heeded his words, he began to despair of the masses turning from their evil ways. However, he felt that sooner or later a creative minority would begin to understand what God wanted. These would in time become the leaven in the lump, renewing in mankind a more dedicated devotion to the will of the Lord. As a result of this faith, Isaiah named his first-born son "Shear-jashub," which literally means "a remnant shall return."

In 735 B.C. the kingdoms of Israel and Syria to the north joined forces to remove themselves from the threat of complete domination by Assyria. To strengthen their cause they called upon Judah to participate in a mutual assistance pact. When Judah's king, Ahaz, refused the offer, preferring neutrality, these two states moved upon Judah in an attempt to force her to become a part of the alliance. They took a position not without parallel in our contemporary era: "To be my friend you must be the enemy of my enemy." Under these circumstances King Ahaz was greatly tempted to call upon Assyria for protection.

During this emergency situation, Isaiah, taking Shear-jashub with him, went to counsel with the king. He found Ahaz out inspecting the city's water supply—a resource of the greatest importance should Jerusalem become besieged. Referring to Syria and Israel, Isaiah admonished Judah: "Take heed, be quiet, do not fear, and do not let your heart be faint because of these two smoldering stumps of firebrands" (7:4). Isaiah encouraged the king to place his faith in the security that God would provide him if he led his nation in the paths of righteousness. If Judah instead depended upon Assyria for safety, she was doomed.

Perhaps one can appreciate the boldness of Isaiah's act if he imagines a respected national leader visiting our President during the height of the Cuban crisis, cautioning against rash action and recommending that he place his faith in righteous conduct. Then he might add:"By the way, Mr. President, this is my son 'Somebody-Shall-Be-Left' "!

To make his message even more striking, Isaiah named his next son "Maher-shalal-hash-baz" ("speeding to the spoil, hastening to the prey"). Those who think preachers' children are handicapped should reserve their pity for prophets' progeny!

Nevertheless Isaiah's warning went unheeded. Ahaz chose to send emissaries to the Assyrian king, Tiglath-pileser, pledging homage in exchange for Judah's defense. Gold and silver from the temple and palace accompanied the king's ambassadors as a persuasive tribute. Revelation of the plotted revolt against Assyria was all the excuse that Tiglath-pileser needed to march into northern Israel in 734 B.C., occupying the territory east of the Jordan and reducing the rest of the kingdom to a tiny Assyrian vassal. Two years later Syria also was defeated with the capture of Damascus. In 721 B.C. the northern kingdom went out of existence and became an Assyrian province.

Thus Judah's position was little improved as a result of the bargain she made. She lost two buffer states between herself and the major power of the day; she was now under the suzerainty of Assyria to whom she had to pay an annual tribute; and to make matters worse she fell under the corrupting influence of Assyrian religion. Ahaz even went so far as to install in the holy temple at Jerusalem a pagan altar modeled after a similar Assyrian piece he had admired on a trip to Damascus.

At this turn of events, Isaiah disgustedly went into seclusion with his family and a few disciples. He was out of public view during the balance of the reign of Ahaz.

Shortly after Hezekiah's ascendancy to the throne, Judah was again faced with a difficult choice. The cities of Philistia, prodded by Egypt and Ethiopia, attempted to free themselves from Sargon II, then the Assyrian monarch. In doing so, they sought support from Judah. Isaiah was strongly opposed to Judah's joining the alliance, and to dramatically demonstrate his objection, he walked naked for three years about the city of Jerusalem. This was to warn his fellow citizens that they would become captives and slaves if they took part in the revolt. No doubt Isaiah's behavior was an embarrassment to government officials as well as to his countrymen, just as today when demonstrators march with placards for peace or racial justice, those in power may be embarrassed and passersby may wish to dissociate themselves from "those radicals."

Isaiah was convinced that Assyria in time would be overthrown. Judah, he felt, should submit to Assyrian rule quietly and trustfully, waiting for that time when God, the Ruler of history, would act to deliver her from oppression. Therefore, the prophet denounced the leaders of Judah who "go down to Egypt for help" and "who trust in chariots." Instead should they not "look to the Holy One of Israel" and "consult the Lord"?

Like the first President of the United States, Isaiah seems to be warning against "entangling alliances" which may in themselves offer no security but instead involve a nation unnecessarily in adventures not in her own interest. G. G. D. Kilpatrick interprets Isaiah as saying here: " 'The truth is that God is the Lord of history, and until you recognize that, until you believe that his power is greater than man's, and that the defeat of the enemies of his purpose is his concern, your clever diplomacy is futile.' "[1] In this instance Hezekiah accepted the advice of Isaiah. Thus, when the commander-in-chief of Sargon "came to Ashdod and fought against it and took it," Judah was spared.

However, the death of Sargon II in 705 B.C. gave the signal to the restless cities of Babylonia and Philistia, supported by Egypt, to make a concerted attempt to throw off the yoke of Assyria. Conceding to Babylonian overtures, King Hezekiah unfortunately agreed to join the rebellion.

Sennacherib, now king of Assyria, marched southward in 701 B.C. to smash the revolt. Following a siege he took the Judean city of Lachish and made it into his new base for operations against King Hezekiah.

At this point Isaiah began to look upon Assyria as the rod of God's anger—the means by which the Lord was exercising his judgment against Judah for her perverseness. Isaiah did not mean to imply that Assyria's behavior was approved by God, for she herself would be punished in due time. But meanwhile God would make use of Assyria to discipline his wayward child Judah. For God was indeed the Lord of all history and his hand was "stretched out over *all* nations."

These were difficult days for Judah. Dozens of her fortified cities were laid waste, and as a climax Sennacherib besieged Jerusalem, shutting up Hezekiah "like a caged bird." Hezekiah was so frightened that he sent a message to the king of Assyria's headquarters begging Assyria's withdrawal and promising, "Whatever you impose on me I will bear." The tribute imposed was harsh indeed: "Judah was forced to turn over to Sennacherib three hundred talents of silver, thirty talents of gold, and costly palace and temple treasures, as well as the king's daughters, his harem, and his male and female musicians."[2]

Even so, it is difficult to understand why Sennacherib withdrew without destroying Jerusalem. A plague afflicting the Assyrian forces has been suggested (2 Kings 19:35). Perhaps domestic difficulties made necessary his return. Or possibly rumors of a new Babylonian revolt urgently required the presence of his forces.

In any event, Isaiah had reassured Hezekiah concerning the Assyrian king: "By the way that he came, by the same shall he return, and he shall not come into this city, says the LORD" (Isa. 37:34). His faith and counsel were justified, for Sennacherib never did capture Jerusalem, and the city was spared for another century.

Isaiah was greatly disappointed that the people did not attribute their unexpected deliverance to the hand of God. For the people of Jerusalem did not gather in the temple for thanksgiving but upon the housetops, shouting, singing, and dancing, giving expression to their relief in wild revelry. All they seemed to care about was their own safety.

Isaiah did not claim to know what would eventually happen to the people of Judah. But he firmly believed that God, at the helm of history, would make provision through a faithful remnant for that day of peace he envisioned—when men would "beat their swords into plowshares, and their spears into pruning hooks" and not "learn war any more."

ISAIAH'S MESSAGE FOR THE MODERN ERA

The eighth-century prophet of Jerusalem spoke about matters of great consequence in a specific historical situation. He was not prophesying for our benefit in the twentieth century. Yet, because mankind is beset with many of the same problems, and bedevils itself as a result of the same human frailties, much of what Isaiah said still arrests our attention. The names of the nations, the political leaders, and the specific situations have all changed outwardly, but the words of the prophet continue to speak the truth.

What are the major ideas found in chapters 1 to 39 which need to be reiterated today?

The prophet had complete confidence in the judgment and victory of the Lord of history. God was the Ruler of the universe and no man could overrule him. This is a lesson modern man needs to learn: one can ignore God but not escape from him. He is sovereign Power in the world and he has unlimited tenure of office. His existence does not depend upon our vote of confidence.

Today we may be less inclined to think of God as intervening at every point in history as Isaiah did. God may not use wicked nations as his holy instruments, but his judgment allows all nations to reap what they have sown. His long-suffering mercy still blesses us, and his ultimate victory is yet assured.

Isaiah incorporated ethical content into his concept of the holiness of God. God's holiness was not to be found in his unapproachability, in his "wholly otherness," but in his absolute righteousness. As his character is grounded in righteousness, so he demands justice, purity, and nobility of spirit from the children of men.

Today it is not enough to think of God primarily as a comforting presence. Such a God would not, for Isaiah, embody the full meaning of holiness. Rather the ethical demands of the Holy One of Israel should make us uncomfortable as well. As someone has said, the true gospel is one which "comforts the disturbed and disturbs the comfortable." One for whom the presence of God means being coddled by an indulgent Father is not likely to possess a humble and contrite heart. Only the moral exaction of " . . . be perfect, as your heavenly Father is perfect" can prevent smugness and evoke penitence.

Isaiah was wary of basing security policy primarily in alliances and military might. Within a year or two the United States is scheduled to have completed plans for a multilateral naval atomic force operated through NATO. Considering that this action will permit Western Germany to be one of the powers with a finger on the atomic trigger, and knowing the Soviet Union's great fear of Germany, there remains much doubt whether this new arrangement will further a peaceful accommodation with the U.S.S.R.

Also one wonders how much the ever-increasing stockpile of atomic weapons adds to our security. True, they do add to our overkill capacity. But now that we have such redundant strength that we can destroy the major population and industrial centers of the Soviet Union many times over, how much is enough?[3]

It would seem that only as we enhance the security of the whole world will the United States be truly secure. This means that we can no longer concentrate on policies which *appear* to safeguard our own vital interests yet ignore the security interests of other nations.

Each man must accept personal responsibility for the plight of society. Our contemporary nuclear dilemma is compounded by the feeling of helplessness which weighs upon many persons once they realize the frightening power of nuclear weapons. As the late President Kennedy stated at American University on June 10,

1963: "A single nuclear weapon contains almost ten times the explosive force delivered by all the Allied air forces in the Second World War." In the face of this magnitude of power we may be tempted to believe that individual action is as futile as shaking one's fist at a hurricane.

But Isaiah engaged in his one-man mission even when confronted with the imminent grim prospect of annihilation. Surely the assumption of personal responsibility today by disciplined individuals could meet with no greater discouragement than he faced.

Late in the summer of 1961, when a bill to create an Arms Control and Disarmament Agency was pending before Congress, few thought the measure had a chance to pass before adjournment. But many responsible Americans poured letters, telegrams, and phone calls into Washington. As a result, in the closing days of Congress the bill passed 5 to 1 in both the Senate and the House. Thus today we have an agency within the government making the necessary studies, hammering out the policies, and contracting for the research which are absolute prerequisites to a safeguarded disarmament treaty.

Deliverance from catastrophe should be used creatively. When the Assyrian siege was lifted, Isaiah deplored the light-footed gaiety and light-headed escapism of the populace. It seemed to him a time for thanksgiving, penitence, and seeking for new directions which would extricate Judah from back-to-back crises.

One cannot compare the relationship of tiny Judah vis-à-vis mighty Assyria with that of the United States vis-à-vis the Soviet Union except perhaps in one aspect: the creative use of a crisis aftermath. Surely in the resolution of the Cuban crisis a reprieve was granted humanity. The God of history delivered both pagan and believer from utter destruction. How is the reprieve being used? If it means only returning to "business as usual" or escaping to frivolities that erase from our minds all serious concerns, then the "nuclear sword of Damocles" has already begun its descent. On the other hand, if more persons are moved to act as though their only real shelter is peace, giving their dedicated attention to the agonizing problems before us, then there is hope indeed.

Selections from First Isaiah

THE FALL OF THE FAITHFUL   1:21-23

How the faithful city
   has become a harlot,
   she that was full of justice!
Righteousness lodged in her,
   but now murderers.
Your silver has become dross,
   your wine mixed with water.
Your princes are rebels
   and companions of thieves.
Every one loves a bribe
   and runs after gifts.
They do not defend the fatherless,
   and the widow's cause does not come to them.

A COMING ERA OF PEACE   2:2-4

It shall come to pass in the latter days
   that the mountain of the house of the LORD
shall be established as the highest of the mountains,
   and shall be raised above the hills;
and all the nations shall flow to it,
   and many peoples shall come, and say:
"Come, let us go up to the mountain of the LORD,
   to the house of the God of Jacob;
that he may teach us his ways
   and that we may walk in his paths."
For out of Zion shall go forth the law,
   and the word of the LORD from Jerusalem.
He shall judge between the nations,
   and shall decide for many peoples;
and they shall beat their swords into plowshares,

and their spears into pruning hooks;
nation shall not lift up sword against nation,
    neither shall they learn war any more.

THE PROUD BROUGHT LOW   2:12-15, 17-19

For the LORD of hosts has a day
    against all that is proud and lofty,
    against all that is lifted up and high;
against all the cedars of Lebanon,
    lofty and lifted up;
    and against all the oaks of Bashan;
against all the high mountains,
    and against all the lofty hills;
against every high tower,
    and against every fortified wall ...
And the haughtiness of man shall be humbled,
    and the pride of men shall be brought low;
    and the LORD alone will be exalted in that day.
And the idols shall utterly pass away.
And men shall enter the caves of the rocks
    and the holes of the ground,
from before the terror of the LORD,
    and from the glory of his majesty,
    when he rises to terrify the earth.

THE HAUGHTY DAUGHTERS OF ZION   3:16-17, 24

The LORD said:
Because the daughters of Zion are haughty
    and walk with outstretched necks,
    glancing wantonly with their eyes,
mincing along as they go,
    tinkling with their feet;
the LORD will smite with a scab
    the heads of the daughters of Zion,
    and the LORD will lay bare their secret parts.
Instead of perfume there will be rottenness;
    and instead of a girdle, a rope;

and instead of well-set hair, baldness;
>and instead of a rich robe, a girding of sackcloth;
instead of beauty, shame.

THE ACQUISITIVE LANDLORDS   5:8-9

Woe to those who join house to house,
>who add field to field,
until there is no more room,
>and you are made to dwell alone
>in the midst of the land.
The LORD of hosts has sworn in my hearing:
"Surely many houses shall be desolate,
>large and beautiful houses, without inhabitant."

HEROES AT DRINKING   5:11, 20-23

Woe to those who rise early in the morning,
>that they may run after strong drink,
who tarry late into the evening
>till wine inflames them! ...
Woe to those who call evil good
>and good evil,
who put darkness for light
>and light for darkness,
who put bitter for sweet
>and sweet for bitter!
Woe to those who are wise in their own eyes,
>and shrewd in their own sight!
Woe to those who are heroes at drinking wine,
>and valiant men in mixing strong drink,
who acquit the guilty for a bribe,
>and deprive the innocent of his right!

ISAIAH'S VISION   6:1-8

In the year that King Uzziah died I saw the Lord sitting upon
a throne, high and lifted up; and his train filled the temple.
Above him stood the seraphim; each had six wings: with two he

covered his face, and with two he covered his feet, and with two he flew. And one called to another and said:

"Holy, holy, holy is the LORD of hosts;
the whole earth is full of his glory."

And the foundations of the thresholds shook at the voice of him who called, and the house was filled with smoke. And I said: "Woe is me! For I am lost; for I am a man of unclean lips, and I dwell in the midst of a people of unclean lips; for my eyes have seen the King, the LORD of hosts!"

Then flew one of the seraphim to me, having in his hand a burning coal which he had taken with tongs from the altar. And he touched my mouth, and said: "Behold, this has touched your lips; your guilt is taken away, and your sin forgiven." And I heard the voice of the Lord saying, "Whom shall I send, and who will go for us?" Then I said, "Here am I! Send me."

THE ROD OF GOD'S ANGER 10:5-6

Ah, Assyria, the rod of my anger,
    the staff of my fury!
against a godless nation I send him,
    and against the people of my wrath I command him,
to take spoil and seize plunder,
    and to tread them down like the mire of the streets.

THE ILL FATE OF LEGALISM 28:13

Therefore the word of the LORD will be to them
    precept upon precept, precept upon precept,
    line upon line, line upon line,
    here a little, there a little;
that they may go, and fall backward,
    and be broken, and snared, and taken.

DEPENDENCE UPON A GRACIOUS GOD 30:12-15, 18

Therefore thus says the Holy One of Israel,
"Because you despise this word,

and trust in oppression and perverseness,
and rely on them;
therefore this iniquity shall be to you
like a break in a high wall, bulging out, and about to
collapse,
whose crash comes suddenly, in an instant;
and its breaking is like that of a potter's vessel
which is smashed so ruthlessly
that among its fragments not a sherd is found
with which to take fire from the hearth,
or to dip up water out of the cistern."
For thus said the Lord GOD, the Holy One of Israel,
"In returning and rest you shall be saved;
in quietness and in trust shall be your strength." . . .
Therefore the LORD waits to be gracious to you;
therefore he exalts himself to show mercy to you.
For the LORD is a God of justice;
blessed are all those who wait for him.

THOSE WHO TRUST IN CHARIOTS   31:1, 3

Woe to those who go down to Egypt for help
and rely on horses,
who trust in chariots because they are many
and in horsemen because they are very strong,
but do not look to the Holy One of Israel
or consult the LORD! . . .
The Egyptians are men, and not God;
and their horses are flesh, and not spirit.
When the LORD stretches out his hand,
the helper will stumble, and he who is helped will fall,
and they will all perish together.

Isaiah—A Wise Statesman for Our Modern Era

THE "FAITHFUL" CITY (1:21)

The faithful city has become a harlot.
Senators sanction insobriety
    in the shadow of your Capitol dome.
You take the bloom off the cherry blossom festival by turning
    a joyous celebration into a common brawl.
At the opening of Congress each day,
    the chaplain's fervent prayers on your behalf
    bounce off the newspapers in which you bury your faces.
Liquor is delivered to your offices in unmarked containers,
    as anonymous as campaign gifts
    to encourage oil depletion votes.
Unanimity prevails in voting billions for defense,
    but debate drones on over a few millions for peace research.
Your beloved capital city wins a prize for juvenile delinquency,
    claims the championship for alcohol consumption,
    forces an unemployed man to desert his wife
        so she can collect ADC payments.
Your schools teach space-age children with ancient texts.
Yet you Congressmen jealously guard your prerogatives
    against District home rule.
You proclaim self-determination for all peoples,
    except those who dwell close to the seats of your power.

SWORDS INTO PLOWSHARES (2:2-4)

And it shall come to pass in the latter days
    men shall catch a vision of God exalted,
    and many peoples shall gather together in a high place.

He shall judge between the nations
  and his judgments shall be their law;
   and they shall beat their swords into plowshares,
    their spears into pruning hooks,
  their atom bombs into useful sources of energy,
    for the good of all of God's children.

PRIDE BROUGHT LOW   (2:12, 17-19)

O people of God, come, let us walk out of the shadows,
  and into the Light shining from heaven.
For the Lord of hosts has a day
  against all that is proud and lofty,
  against all that is lifted up and high,
  against all Empire State buildings,
  against every powerful space craft,
  against all bomb tests everywhere,
  against every Berlin wall,
  against all multilateral atomic naval forces,
  against all rattling of rockets and brandishing of missiles,
  against all stockpiling of stocks and bonds.
And the haughtiness of man shall be humbled,
  and the pride of men shall be brought low;
  and the Lord alone will be exalted in that day.
All *idols shall utterly pass away.*
For on that day *men shall enter the caves of the rocks.*
They shall go down into the tombs they think are shelters,
  fleeing from the terror they have created themselves.
In that day the stocks which they have preserved
  will be investments in burning ashes;
their proud sleek Babels will tilt
  like the leaning tower of Pisa;
their walls to keep men in
  will be easily trespassed by rats in the ruins.
The Scriptures will be fulfilled among them:
  they that take up the missile shall go down by the missile.
For men will flee, from the love of God they are to express,
  to inflict terror on their fellows.

THIS GENERATION'S DAUGHTERS (3:16-26)

O daughters of this generation, preoccupied with vanity,
   doing the twist as you mince along,
   donning spike heels that display the ankles but destroy the
     arches,
wearing sunglasses, not to shade the eyes,
   but to conceal wanton sidelong glances,
eyes painted wide, but not wide enough
   to discern the signs of the times.
Will you lengthen your skirts; or carry a baton to twirl?
You who mouth sweet words of freedom,
   but allow Paris and New York to dictate conformity,
because of your haughtiness and foolishness,
the Lord has sworn:
   That day will come when, *instead of perfume,*
     there will be the odor of decay,
   instead of high heels, dirty bare feet,
   instead of a girdle, a rope,
   instead of well-tinted hair, snarled dishwater-blonde,
   instead of a dress of signboard scarlet, torn denim.
Awake! that that day may be held back.
Complete your emancipation:
   Become human—let the china doll walk off the shelf;
     dress modestly—carry surprises to your marriage bed;
     overcome your obsession with appearance—
       pass by a mirror without looking in.
Let others know who *you* are, unbarricaded by beauty parlor
   hours.
Cultivate interest in the vital issues of the day,
   not those which lead so quickly to sophisticated boredom.

POSSESSORS POSSESSED (5:8)

Woe unto those who, with unending avarice, add property to
     property,
   until they are possessed by what they own.
The Lord of hosts has sworn in my hearing:
They shall count houses at midnight instead of sheep.

"Which roof leaks?" "Will he pay the rent?"
  "Shall I put the back forty in the land bank?"
"Are the expenses for the new tenant justified?"
  "Can I unload the land I got stung on?"
"Will they reroute the highway my motel fronts on?"
  "Will Negroes move into my subdivision?"

THE DRINKING HEROES   (5:22)

Why are you *heroes at drinking* beer? *valiant men in mixing*
    martinis?
You know that liquor adversely affects the mind,
  that remarkable faculty which elevates you above the animal.
Party-givers, must you loosen up the crowd with a cocktail?
Gracious hosts, would you say frankly to your guests:
  "You are a stupid bore in your natural state.
  Here, have a few drinks to overcome your unbearable dull-
      ness,
  to stir up the dormant brilliance of your personality!"
Do you advise moderation in using a substance whose first effect
  weakens the power to stop?
Consult your five million alcoholics.
  Did not each plan to be a moderate drinker?
Will my voice go unheeded, drowned out by raucous drunken
    laughter?
Then know the consequences of your folly!
Build your mammoth hospitals for alcoholic priests.
Crowd your mental institutions with the chronic whiskey-
    sodden.
Let blood run down the hills of your highways,
  blood, your beverage mixer for martinis.
Let stewardesses be glorified
  for pushing drinks on airliners.
Let your juveniles get beered up
  for a delinquent spree.
Let your teen-age girls bear illegitimate children
  whose nameless father is gin.
Let your criminals commit unthinkable crimes,

not contemplated in sober moments.
Pour the rich talent of your writers
  down the sewer with their vomit.

HOW TO AVOID THE GOSPEL

Your prophets must write fiction;
  truth outright is too painful to your hearts.
You place the word "THINK"
  above your IBM machines.
But on your pulpits have you engraved "ENTERTAIN"?
Is there something sacrilegious
  about loving the Lord your God with all your mind?
Your theologians stress eschatology
  and strip bare the ethics of Christ.
They are like shrewd taxpayers looking for loopholes.

THE CALL OF A MAN   (6:1-8)

In the year the Space Age was born,
I had a vision of God,
  not through a glass darkly, but face to face.
I sat in church that morning,
  the morning his presence filled the sanctuary.
So overpowering was the experience,
  I was oblivious to others in the congregation.
The all-embracing presence of God
  was closer than the people in my pew.
His thereness was unmistakable.
We had sung a joyful hymn of praise,
  the choir's anthem had lifted my soul out of my body;
  the minister was reading from the Word which suddenly
    became flesh
A great Force swept through the sanctuary.
It was as though in that instant of eternity, past and future
    merged;
  and I knew these people, God's people, intimately;
  and all shared in the divine secret and blessing.
We knew his holiness and he overlooked our frailty.

It was then we were aware that the Lord our God was calling
      us
   to some majestic task—
as he called Moses in a burning bush,
   the prophets from tending their sheep,
   Jesus from a carpenter's bench,
   and Saul on a Damascus road.
"I'm not good enough," I mumbled, and slumped in my seat.
Perhaps the pastor could represent us,
   or the lay leader, George Johnson.
   Let George do it.
But the Spirit could not be shaken.
For a Voice spoke forth, more ultimatum than request:
   "Whom shall I send, and who will go for us?"
There was no escaping, for the Voice boomed out
   from all four walls, directly at me.
Every face, now so apparent, was turned in my direction.
In tones so steady I barely claimed them for my own,
   my voice replied, *"Here am I! Send me."*

SLEEPING SPIRITS, AWAKE!   (10:5-6)

   Ah, Russia, *the rod of my anger!*
   Ah, Soviets, *the staff of my fury!*
   Against a godless nation I send you,
      and against the people of my disappointment I command
         you.
   Though you are wicked and atheistic yourselves,
      I tolerate your power as judgment
   to frustrate those who confess me with their lips,
      but ignore me in their daily pursuits.
   For you are my spur to stab the flesh,
      that sleeping spirits may awaken from dreams—
   dreams that they can utterly deny me,
      and walk in the pleasure of their hearts,
      that science will prosper them,
      that shelters will protect them,
      that dollars will save them,

that cosmetics will keep them young,
and the government will keep them when they are old,
that they can put God in a safe-deposit box
　　at the corner of Main and Elm.
　Now will they examine the truth?
　　Look to the faith that is in them?
　　Discover the Power that could permeate them?
　　Respond to the Love that would again make them human,
　　　raise them from animal passions,
　　　　and lower them from their pedestal of self-worship?

WHAT GOD REQUIRES

Thus says the Lord:
　I delight not in your cash-laden collection plates.
　Your pretentious churches are an abomination;
　　they vary monotonously from Gothic provincial to factory
　　　modern.
　On Christmas your gifts are more important
　　than the Gift of God.
　On Easter you parade your finery before the Deity.
　I do not look upon what is on your head,
　　but what is in your heart.
　Your Sabbaths are not holy days but holidays.
　　They exhaust the body and corrupt the soul.
　　Bleary-eyed and footsore you turn to Monday.
　Do not appear before me with a guilt offering
　　as your price of admission,
　or with fashionable attire to entitle you to the best places
　　in air-conditioned pews comfortable enough to sleep in.
　Air-condition your musty souls; purify your spirits; humble
　　　your prideful hearts.
　Enter your sanctuary prepared to hear the Word of the Lord.
　Sing the great hymns without hypocrisy.
　When the minister lifts supplication on your behalf,
　　read not the bulletin,
　　nor count the holes in the accoustical tile.
　When the Word is proclaimed for the edification of your soul,

let not mother prepare next week's menus,
or father peruse his "accounts due,"
or sister choose her dress for the prom,
or brother replay Saturday's game.
Let the mind wander only where the conscience leads and the
Spirit moves,
watering the desert places of the soul.
Go forth determined to do good:
to understand the misunderstood,
to overlook the mistakes of the mistaken,
to love the unloved,
to forgive the unforgiven.
Let your heart be immersed in the love of God,
buoyed up like a swimmer in the salty sea.

INEFFECTIVENESS OF CONTAINMENT

Let the Russian bear, in hibernation for centuries,
come out of his cave hungry for prowl.
Let the hunter find out he can't slay him,
or place him in a cage at the zoo,
though armed with tactical atomic weapons,
and the nets of radar equipment.
He shall leap over the pits of containment,
and seek berries and honey afar.

THE NEW AMERICAN ISOLATIONISM

Draw near, O America, to hear.
In the thirties you proudly set yourself apart
from involvement with the world;
but in the sixties you are thoroughly committed
from Saigon to Istanbul to Caracas.
Yet today you would isolate others
as you once insulated yourself:
by placing an embargo on Cuba
and penalizing unco-operative nations;
by discouraging trade with China
and preventing her UN admission.

Long ago you fenced in the Soviet Union
   through non-acceptance in incipient years.
Yet in time you were forced to admit
   her existence as a major power.
On your Archives building you have carved:
   "What is past is prologue."
Thus, can the New Isolationism succeed
   when the Old so clearly demonstrated its failure?
Will you end your days alone
   with a brimming cup of bitterness
   and no companion nation with which to drink?

THE WOLF WITH THE LAMB (11:6-9)

Hasten that day when none shall *hurt or destroy*
   in all my holy mountain,
and *the earth shall be full of the knowledge of the Lord*
   as the waters cover the sea,
when the beasts of the field and the birds of the air
   shall know their freedom,
   and all shall dwell in a land of peace.
The wolf shall dwell with the lamb, the leopard shall lie down
     with the kid,
   and the bear cubs shall not disturb the eagle's nest.

A TALE OF TWO CITIES (13—19)

East Berliners! Do you not know
   that man was born with wings in his heart?
That no wall can contain him,
   no barbed wire catch him in its web?
What he cannot jump over
   he will ram through.
What he cannot swim across
   he will tunnel under.
You have named your country "Democratic,"
   yet your people fear the secret police
   and speak in curfew tones on street corners.
Though your Karl Marx Allee is impressive,

it bears as little traffic as a back alley.
A new city cries to be erected
  on rubble in which no half-brick fits another.
The Zone regime jams radio
while in the West there rises
  an international center of culture, education, and truth.
The Wall proclaims to other peoples: "Keep out!"
The Free City says to foreign artists and writers: "Come in!"
West Berlin is a shelf
  in a showcase requiring two shelves with no war trophies.
Bark seeks to cover the scar left by a severed limb;
  how long can hate divide what all nature would unite and
    heal?

THE FREE WORLD   (21—23)

The oracle concerning the free world:
  O weep, Patrick Henry; shed tears, Thomas Jefferson;
    groan in the grave, Tom Paine!
For the principles you held dear have been perverted.
  Your beloved country does not know her mother.
She has the brow of a harlot, unfaithful to her heritage.
  She would consort with all who are enemies of her enemy,
  though they be not friends of the precepts
    her tradition has upheld.
O America, favorite daughter of my bosom,
  you speak of looking toward a concert of free nations.
But what do you mean by "free"?
  France, cradle of European liberty,
    dominated by a De Gaulle with dictatorial powers?
  Portugal, oppressor of Angola,
    whose subjugated people seek genuine independence?
  Spain, persecutor of Protestants,
    to whose military you give aid and training, entrenching
    Franco in power?
  Taiwan, where your generous assistance
    keeps ten million Formosans under the hated heel of
    Chiang Kai-shek?

Korea, where a costly war fought for freedom
   has left our beneficiaries the dubious privilege of life
      under a minority-elected military leader?
South Vietnam, that "bastion of the Free World,"
   where thousands forced from ancestral lands are herded
      into hamlets?
For this, the freedom you claim to possess
   shall be eaten away by fanatics,
who, in the name of anti-Communism,
   would banish liberty from the land,
   and nonconformity from the nation.
Stay your anger, O Lord!
For my people are like an adolescent prince ascended to the
      throne.
Spare them, O God, till they reach the wisdom of maturity.

SEPARATION—WHITE FROM BLACK

The oracle concerning race:
   Why do you make so much of your separation, white from
      black?
   I have never told you I would separate you,
      except as sheep from goats.
   And why have you had so much strife along Route 40?
   Should not access routes between New York and Washington
      be just as free as those to West Berlin?
   How can you expect, America, to get along
      with the two-thirds of the world that is colored
      if you can't get along among yourselves?
   Your churches reject kneeling-in Negroes,
      while voicing creeds about the Fatherhood of God.
   And many patriotic Americans believe in the freedom of the
         Negro
      to live next door to somebody else.
   Your "sheriff's spelling bees" held at polling places
      cover up a loosely veiled travesty of justice.
   Too many of your restaurants are granted licenses to serve the
         public,

then proceed to put up their signs
"We reserve the right to refuse service."
Why do you make so much of your separation, white from
black?
White women go to the beauty parlor to get their hair curled,
and Negro women go to get their hair straightened.
White women carefully apply their suntan lotion
and Negro women apply their bleaching creams.
A white man is saved from death by Negro blood of his same
type.
For I made of one blood all the nations of the earth,
and every Christian is called to be color-blind.

COMMUNISM

The oracle concerning Communism:
O nation of the hammer and sickle!
Would you use the hammer
to pound propaganda into the minds of your people?
And the sickle to cut down all
who will not conform to the current Kremlin line?
When your five-year plan fails,
you convert it to a seven-year plan;
when that falters,
you shift to a twenty-year plan.
When will your people be aware,
and respond not to Stalin's stick,
or Khrushchev's elusive carrot?
O virgin lands of Siberia!
When will the sower overtake the reaper
since the reaper cannot keep up with the sower?
You boast of Communist production,
yet half your livestock is raised on private plots.
You are proud of your mechanization,
yet within the grounds of your Economic Exhibition,
in front of your Heavy Industry Hall,
two weary men cut the grass with long-handled scythes.
Your industry produces the marvel of a sputnik,

but not the simplest object—a ball-point pen.
You are a nation where Tolstoy's genius
  is recognized only in small print,
  and Pasternak is out of print!
I perceive that you have a sense of humor,
  for your censored newspaper is called *Pravda,*
  meaning "truth."
You claim to be a classless society, yet your scientists
  receive ten times your street-sweepers' wages.
Because all your new apartment buildings look the same,
  it would not pay to come home drunk at night,
yet many Muscovites manage this accomplishment,
  requiring forty sobering-up stations in your capital city alone.
Your five-room log houses, topped with three TV aerials,
  tell an unpublicized story of crowded housing conditions.
Your people's clothing is often rumpled
  from storage under beds of closetless apartments.
Your women work on mixing cement and repairing railroad
    tracks,
  on laying brick and tarring roads,
  which proves their emancipation from the inequality of the
    sexes.
You claim to be great advocates of peace,
  but dress your schoolboys in military garb.
You offer to support all wars of national liberation,
  then crush a genuine revolt in nearby Hungary.
You purport to uphold the virtues of materialism,
  yet fear to use your richest natural resource—the free hu-
    man spirit.
For this, your agriculture shall languish,
    and your people shall eat steel;
until the portentous day arrives
  when youth educated in science start to think about politics;
when they begin to know what the outside world knows,
  penetrating an Iron Curtain that can keep people in,
  but not ideas out.

"THE SPIRIT GIVETH LIFE"   (28:13)

Oracle to the ministers:

> *Therefore the word of the Lord will be to them*
> *line upon line, table upon table, figures upon figures.*

You preachers know all the statistics, from pastors' salaries
   to memberships of churches.

Must you all get the bishop's eye?

Does your ministry have to be judged by comparative annual
      reports?

Must you pile member on member, budget on budget,
   building on building, to be "successful"?

Would not other vital statistics reveal the real strength of a
      church?

> How many members walked out on sermons last year?
> How many pounds of clothing were contributed to overseas
>   relief?
> How many marriages were kept from going on the rocks?
> How many of your youth are candidates for the ministry?
> How many missionaries are supported through special gifts?

BARREN PLANS AND ALLIANCES   (30:1–2)

> *"Woe to the rebellious children," says the Lord,*
> *"who carry out a plan, but not mine;*
> *and who make a league, but not of my spirit,"*
> who invade Cuba without seeking my counsel,
> who engage in illegal overflights without asking my advice.

They have their plans:

> How to become rich on real estate working weekends;
> How to retire and loaf before 30;
> How to have a tranquil soul and not give a hang
>   if the world goes to hell.

They have their alliances:

> a SEATO guaranteed to make any Asian war a "white for-
>   eign intrusion,"
> a NATO dominated by Germans not known for restraint in
>   launching war.

Their plans are not the Divine Plan.
In their alliances I cannot be their Ally.

THE CIRCLE OF DEATH (30:12-14)

Thus says the Lord:
Because you despise this word,
and trust in oppression and perverseness,
and rely on them;
therefore this iniquity shall be to you
like the smashing of a tool into dozens of pieces,
so minute that not a piece is found large enough for a
hammer,
or sharp enough for a chisel.
Some speak lightly of your atomic destruction,
claiming your society could be rebuilt in a few years.
Rebuild your industry with machines!
We have no machines.
Rebuild your machines with tools!
We have no tools.
Rebuild your tools with castings!
We have no castings.
Rebuild your castings with ore!
We have no ore.
Dig your ore!
We have no machines.

RESPONSE TO GOD'S GRACE (30:15, 18)

For thus said the Lord God,
"In returning and rest you shall be saved;
in quietness and in trust shall be your strength."
Therefore the Lord waits to be gracious to you;
therefore he exalts himself to show mercy to you.
For the Lord is a God of justice;
blessed are all those who wait for him.
Is thunder heard in an uninhabited desert?
Can sunshine cause an unplanted garden to grow?

Will the most delicious dinner be served
    to invited guests unarrived?
Can the choicest award be presented
    if the recipient declines?
Neither can God give you his richest blessing,
    unless you are willing to unwrap his gifts.
Wait upon the Lord, and renew your faith.

WOE TO THOSE—   (31)

Woe to those who exalt sex,
    who enrich themselves by inflaming the passions,
    who publish pornographic literature,
    who transform a beautiful woman into a goddess of love
    and exploit her through magazines, movies, and television.
Therefore your youth grow lax in morals,
    the bonds of marriage are loosened,
    and crimes of lust abound in your cities.
Woe to those who carve upon their marble buildings,
    "Equal justice under law,"
yet they close the voting booth against my people of color.
They extend not the protection of enforcement officials,
    nor grant equal treatment by judge or jury.
Woe to those who preach democracy
    yet they shut their schools rather than admit the Negro,
    and bomb his churches when he dares protest.
Woe to those who add air base to air base,
    who encircle the globe with their bombers,
    and plant their missiles on reluctant soil.
Yet shall they feel no security,
    for all their farflung armaments.
Woe to those who talk glibly of peace,
    yet they brandish the threat of annihilation.
Therefore they shall live in fear,
    and none shall trust them
    until they learn to trust in my Spirit,
                        says the Lord of the universe.

THE PLEASANT LITTLE WAR

Your military leaders say:
Let us never again have a general war;
  for an all-out nuclear war would destroy civilization.
But let us be prepared for limited wars—
  wars in which nuclear weapons would be used on military
    targets only;
  conventional wars in which only tactical nuclear arms would
    be brought into play;
  wars in outer space where the earth could be spared.
"Let us not give up war," said the general.
  "Let us keep it within bounds,
  a gentlemen's affair."
Thus says the Lord:
How can you establish rules for modern war?
Military drills may have their "war games,"
but once the battle is joined,
  and the days and the months pile bitterness upon hostility,
  then the shock of bombing open cities wears thin;
  the Coventrys become Dresdens and Hamburgs;
  and the Pearl Harbors, Hiroshimas;
  and no open guilt is admitted.
Can you count on a "little nuclear war,"
  or a conflict of military forces only?
Such strategy based on a "friendly exchange"
  taxes the imagination beyond wondering.
Escalation would surely take place.
The vengeance that is mine would be taken by men
  into their own hands.
Remember, O man!
The ultimate weapon has been used in every major war.
In World War I,
  poison gas;
in World War II,
  the atomic bomb.

THE RUSSIAN ORTHODOX CHURCH*

An oracle concerning the Russian Orthodox Church:
    It was the week of the October Revolution.
    Russian Orthodox leaders were gathered in solemn assembly.
    Many ecclesiastical matters graced the agenda,
        while violence stalked the land,
           and blood ran free in the palaces and streets of the nation;
        while a cause was born
        that would shake the foundations of the world.
    For days the priests debated; the hierarchy held spirited
           discussions
        on a most important issue before them,
        plaguing their commission on ritual.
    "What color stoles," they queried one another,
        "shall we wear during the seasons of the year?"
    Affable priests, silent prophets, and simple peasants
        go down to the pit together.
    The priests are wearing black,
        and the season is one of mourning.

    It is a quarter of a century later.
    Russian church leaders are again in assembly.
    They gather together at New Delhi with the World Council of
        Churches.

* It is only fair to say that the Sobor, or church assembly, *did* understand that the Revolution threatened the position of the Russian Orthodox Church. However, rather than being concerned with the problems facing the peasants and workers, problems which spawned the Revolution, the Sobor focused its attention upon the re-establishment of the Patriarchate so that the church might be more effective in dealing with the state as it sought to protect its own interests. The church favored the continuance of the war and opposed peace talks with Germany—this despite the fact that both soldiers and citizenry were sick of the conflict. Recommendations were sent to the Constituent Assembly (never successfully convened) which largely centered around maintenance of ecclesiastical prerogatives, such as: the tax-free status of church property; the continuance of parochial schools; the right of the church to support from state funds.

Control of the Sobor was in the hands of the ultra-conservative upper clergy most of the time although the liberal minority in the assembly fought a vigorous but losing battle during the early months. Thus, it can be said that the mainstream of church leadership was out of touch with a populace desiring more than status quo. (For a thorough discussion of the spirit and action of the Sobor, see *The Russian Church and the Soviet State* by John Shelton Curtiss, Boston: Little, Brown and Company, 1955, pp. 9-70.)

They are in the fraternal company of Christians from near
    and far,
    brothers who have officially received them,
    together with their thirty million members.
Surely the church is the only institution
    leaping over man-made walls and piercing through Iron
      Curtains
      to embrace, in a fellowship of love, citizens of enemy
      nations.
The debates again are spirited; divergent views emerge.
Yet on this the Russians agree:
    "Communism is a judgment upon us,
    for rendering the gospel irrelevant!"

Can American churches and constituent Christians
become so involved in petty peripheries,
    in building campaigns and finance drives,
    in spaghetti suppers and routine ritual,
that there is no time to be the church,
    to bless mankind as peacemakers,
    to assume our role as "sons of God,"
    to make the gospel relevant to our day?

THE CONTROL OF POWER

How can you handle your mounting power
    unless you turn to another Power,
    who gives direction as well as force?
Your atomic physicists estimate there are extant in the world
    sixty thousand megatons of nuclear power.
Your population experts estimate there are extant in the world
    three billion inhabitants populating our planet.
Simple arithmetic then reveals
    that in terms of equivalent nuclear power,
There are twenty tons of TNT
    for every man, woman, and child on earth!
In your Fourth of July celebrations,
    you have outlawed dangerous fireworks;
in your state legislatures,

you have established new controls over rifles and pistols.
Yet consider the international community, unable to outlaw
nuclear weapons,
weapons not to maim a few adults or kill a few children,
but which threaten all mankind.
Not only are you unable to eliminate dangerous arms,
but you face the alarming prospect of the imminent spread of
atomic weapons.
Who will be next in the Nuclear Club?
An Israel perpetually feuding with Egypt?
A China immersed in the theory of the inevitability of war?
A Germany which took initiative in two world wars?
Act! Move! Agree! Decide! Turn back from the abyss!

BY WHOSE PRINCIPLES?

Have you not heard the injunction of the Lord?
"If thine enemy hunger, feed him."
Yet there are those among you who say,
"Let them starve, and let hunger be the curse of Com-
munism.
Let us not show mercy and love, but be as cold and calculating
and ruthless as the enemy.
Let's win for a change!"
Is your memory so short?
A man in Central Europe said,
"Let us waste no love on Jews, spare no mercy to captured
Poles.
Blot out the Bible from your mind.
The sword is more important than the Cross."
That man wanted to win, too.
His name was Hitler.
No, saith the Lord, do not adopt the attitudes or ape the
methods
of those who hold an alien philosophy.
What does it profit you, if in the struggle with your adversary,
you become identical with him?

You have your own ideals to promote,
   your own principles to uphold.
It does not take fire to put out fire,
   but water—Living Water.
Is your enemy hungry?
   Feed him.
Does he slander?
   Bless.
Is he hostile?
   Show friendship.
Does he act belligerent?
   Be understanding.
Is his mouth full of lies?
   Speak the truth in love.

THE GIFT OF PEACE

Many gifts have been received by the United Nations
   from the various countries of the world.
Symbolically they adorn the temple of the nations.
There are statues from Greece,
   paintings from Brazil,
   woodcarvings from Indonesia.
But the most impressive symbol enhancing the Parliament of
   Man
   is an empty space—
the dome of the General Assembly, left incomplete
   to signify the unfinished tasks of peace.
Fly a white dove to the dome!
Crown it with a wreath of olive branches!

III | JONAH

Jonah—His Times and Ours

In the latter part of the fourth century B.C. the Jewish people were under Greek rule. Having been subject to a succession of foreign conquerors—Assyria, Babylonia, Persia—the Jews had almost forgotten the concept of God's universal love for all nations. They looked forward to the day when God would exalt them and give vent to his wrath upon their neighbors and over-lords. Judaism had become ingrown, with an emphasis upon legalism, ritual, and the priestly functions.

During this era an anonymous Jewish religious thinker wrote a parable to jolt his countrymen out of their provincialism, to rekindle the missionary zeal of Second Isaiah, to remind them they were chosen by God to be a light to the Gentiles. He took as the central figure of his tale a prophet named Jonah who typified Jewish nationalism and scorn toward heathen nations.

Jonah is commanded by God to go to Nineveh, an Assyrian city noted for its wickedness, to warn the people to repent. But Jonah cares very little about the redemption of any people other than the Israelites. So instead of heading east to Nineveh he sails west toward Tarshish, a Spanish port as far west as ships from Judah ever ventured.

In resisting the call of God, Jonah is subject to a series of calamities—a terrible storm at sea and his well-known episode with the great fish. In the midst of all this, God's insistent call comes once more to Jonah to go to Nineveh and preach to her people so they may change their ways and be spared destruction. This time Jonah heeds the Lord's request. He travels to Nineveh and preaches in the name of God to its wicked inhabitants. "Yet forty days," cries Jonah, "and Nineveh shall be overthrown!"

* Although the book of Jonah was written in the fourth century B.C. and reflects that era, the author appropriated for his main character a relatively obscure prophet, "Jonah, the son of Amittai," who lived in Israel about 785 B.C. (See 2 Kings 14:25). For this reason Jonah is introduced at this point.

Then the unforeseen happens. The Ninevites actually do repent and as a token of their repentance put on sackcloth and ashes. But Jonah does not respond as one would expect a prophet to behave. He is angry and bitter because God has seen fit to show compassion upon these wayward foreigners who have turned from their sin. Far from desiring the salvation of the Ninevites, he had hoped to be an eyewitness to their destruction.

While Jonah sits outside the city waiting to see what action God will take, a vigorous gourd grows up and provides the prophet with shade. When the next day it withers, Jonah is resentful because God has let the comfort-bringing vine perish. The Lord then asks Jonah why, if he had pity upon a shortlived plant, should not God himself take pity upon a city containing thousands of innocent people.

THE MAJOR TEACHING OF JONAH

No pre-Christian biblical book expresses the concept of God's universal love as clearly as does the parable of Jonah. One might draw an interesting comparison with Jesus' parable of the good Samaritan. In both accounts those who ignore God's will were popularly considered the religious leaders of their day—the provincial prophet in Jonah and the priests and Levites of Jesus' story. On the other hand, the people who did God's will—the repentant Ninevites and the good Samaritan—were despised by devout Jews at the time the stories were told.

JONAH'S MESSAGE FOR THE MODERN ERA

The concept of the universal love of God is one which the author of Jonah could well share with our contemporary world. "National self-interest," which is the guideline of the foreign policies of most countries, often runs counter to the expression of sincere compassion for the well-being of other peoples.

For example, the United States allows approximately $2 billion per year for its economic aid program to help answer human needs on our planet. At the same time we provide more than $5 billion annually for our program in unpopulated outer space. While any bill with the word "space" in it tends to jet-propel its way intact through both the House and Senate, the foreign aid bill traditionally is discussed by four committees of Congress and usually has been slashed in varying degrees by each one.

An experience related by Dr. Darrell Randall typifies our attitudes toward world-wide human needs. Dr. and Mrs. Randall, Christian missionaries to Africa, were once traveling by train from Elizabethville to Johannesburg. Their train passed through a section of Africa which periodically suffered severe drought and famine. During these hunger seasons Africans often had to live on roots until the next crop was harvested. At supper time they pulled into the station of a small town in that destitute area. The two missionaries were in the dining car enjoying a sumptuous meal. As the train stopped, a crowd of Africans, mostly children, gathered about the dining car and peered hungrily through the glass. Needless to say, the Randalls could not enjoy their food under these circumstances. At the suggestion of the porter they did what most sensitive persons would do—they reached up and pulled down the curtain.

Looking back, Dr. Randall concluded that this is the way, too often, we American Christians react to the third of the world which is always hungry. These marginal-living people of Africa, Asia, and Latin America are no longer in ignorance about the world situation. They are very much aware of our abundance. In fact, they are peering through our window. And frequently we pull down the shade so as not to be haunted by our disturbed consciences. However, on the other hand, through government assistance such as Food for Peace and through the missionary and world service efforts of our churches, we can make credible our faith that God's love and mercy extends to all of the children of men.

If we are to give spiritual expression to the universality at the heart of the book of Jonah, we must be concerned about narrowing the gap between the "have" and "have not" nations, but that is not enough. We should also seek to bridge the chasm between East and West. The American Christian should seek every opportunity to express good will toward his brethren in the Soviet Union. One heartening step toward reconciliation was taken when the thirty-million-member Russian Orthodox Church was received into the World Council of Churches in 1961. Thus the church is the only non-governmental institution which embraces in a fellowship of love the citizens of adversary nations.

In March 1963, top leaders of the Russian Orthodox Church were guests of the National Council of Churches in the United States. One day while attending meetings at the Interchurch Center in New York City they were picketed by a right-wing group who felt it was unpatriotic and disloyal to associate with the Russians. In the evening, as the Russian churchmen left a dinner at Riverside Church, they were greeted by more than one hundred students from nearby Union Theological Seminary, who broke into singing "In Christ There Is No East or West."

Edna St. Vincent Millay in her poem "Renascence" wrote:

> The world stands out on either side
> No wider than the heart is wide;
> Above the world is stretched the sky,—
> No higher than the soul is high.[1]

The author of Jonah calls us to widen our hearts and to lift up our souls "to let the face of God shine through."

The Book of Jonah

JONAH FLEES FROM GOD'S CALL

Now the word of the LORD came to Jonah the son of Amittai, saying, "Arise, go to Nineveh, that great city, and cry against it; for their wickedness has come up before me." But Jonah rose to flee to Tarshish from the presence of the LORD. He went down to Joppa and found a ship going to Tarshish; so he paid the fare, and went on board, to go with them to Tarshish, away from the presence of the LORD.

But the LORD hurled a great wind upon the sea, and there was a mighty tempest on the sea, so that the ship threatened to break up. Then the mariners were afraid, and each cried to his god; and they threw the wares that were in the ship into the sea, to lighten it for them. But Jonah had gone down into the inner part of the ship and had lain down, and was fast asleep. So the captain came and said to him, "What do you mean, you sleeper? Arise, call upon your god! Perhaps the god will give a thought to us, that we do not perish."

And they said to one another, "Come, let us cast lots, that we may know on whose account this evil has come upon us." So they cast lots, and the lot fell upon Jonah. Then they said to him, "Tell us, on whose account this evil has come upon us? What is your occupation? And whence do you come? What is your country? And of what people are you?" And he said to them, "I am a Hebrew; and I fear the LORD, the God of heaven, who made the sea and the dry land." Then the men were exceedingly afraid, and said to him, "What is this that you have done!" For the men knew that he was fleeing from the presence of the LORD, because he had told them.

Then they said to him, "What shall we do to you, that the sea may quiet down for us?" For the sea grew more and more tempestuous. He said to them, "Take me up and throw me into the sea; then the sea will quiet down for you; for I know it is because of me that this great tempest has come upon you." Nevertheless the men rowed hard to bring the ship back to land, but they could not, for the sea grew more and more tempestuous against them. Therefore they cried to the LORD, "We beseech thee, O LORD, let us not perish for this man's life, and lay not on us innocent blood; for thou, O LORD, hast done as it pleased thee." So they took up Jonah and threw him into the sea; and the sea ceased from its raging. Then the men feared the LORD exceedingly, and they offered a sacrifice to the LORD and made vows.

IN HIS DISTRESS JONAH REPENTS

And the LORD appointed a great fish to swallow up Jonah; and Jonah was in the belly of the fish three days and three nights.

Then Jonah prayed to the LORD his God from the belly of the fish, saying,

> "I called to the LORD, out of my distress,
>   and he answered me;
> out of the belly of Sheol I cried,
>   and thou didst hear my voice.
> For thou didst cast me into the deep,
>   into the heart of the seas,
>   and the flood was round about me;
> all thy waves and thy billows
>   passed over me.
> Then I said, 'I am cast out
>   from thy presence;
> how shall I again look
>   upon thy holy temple?'
> The waters closed in over me,
>   the deep was round about me;
> weeds were wrapped about my head
>   at the roots of the mountains.
> I went down to the land
>   whose bars closed upon me for ever;
> yet thou didst bring up my life from the Pit,

O LORD my God.
When my soul fainted within me,
    I remembered the LORD;
and my prayer came to thee,
    into thy holy temple.
Those who pay regard to vain idols
    forsake their true loyalty.
But I with the voice of thanksgiving
    will sacrifice to thee;
what I have vowed I will pay.
    Deliverance belongs to the LORD!"

And the LORD spoke to the fish, and it vomited out Jonah upon the dry land.

NINEVEH REPENTS AT JONAH'S PREACHING

Then the word of the LORD came to Jonah the second time, saying, "Arise, go to Nineveh, that great city, and proclaim to it the message that I tell you." So Jonah arose and went to Nineveh, according to the word of the LORD. Now Nineveh was an exceedingly great city, three days' journey in breadth. Jonah began to go into the city, going a day's journey. And he cried, "Yet forty days, and Nineveh shall be overthrown!" And the people of Nineveh believed God; they proclaimed a fast, and put on sackcloth, from the greatest of them to the least of them.

Then tidings reached the king of Nineveh, and he arose from his throne, removed his robe, and covered himself with sackcloth, and sat in ashes. And he made proclamation and published through Nineveh, "By the decree of the king and his nobles: Let neither man nor beast, herd nor flock, taste anything; let them not feed, or drink water, but let man and beast be covered with sackcloth, and let them cry mightily to God; yea, let every one turn from his evil way and from the violence which is in his hands. Who knows, God may yet repent and turn from his fierce anger, so that we perish not?"

When God saw what they did, how they turned from their evil way, God repented of the evil which he had said he would do to them; and he did not do it.

THE REBUKE OF JONAH

But it displeased Jonah exceedingly, and he was angry. And he prayed to the LORD and said, "I pray thee, LORD, is not this what I said when I was yet in my country? That is why I made haste to flee to Tarshish; for I knew that thou art a gracious God and merciful, slow to anger, and abounding in steadfast love, and repentest of evil. Therefore now, O LORD, take my life from me, I beseech thee, for it is better for me to die than to live." And the LORD said, "Do you do well to be angry?" Then Jonah went out of the city and sat to the east of the city, and made a booth for himself there. He sat under it in the shade, till he should see what would become of the city.

And the LORD God appointed a plant, and made it come up over Jonah, that it might be a shade over his head, to save him from his discomfort. So Jonah was exceedingly glad because of the plant. But when dawn came up the next day, God appointed a worm which attacked the plant, so that it withered. When the sun rose, God appointed a sultry east wind, and the sun beat upon the head of Jonah so that he was faint; and he asked that he might die, and said, "It is better for me to die than to live." But God said to Jonah, "Do you do well to be angry for the plant?" And he said, "I do well to be angry, angry enough to die." And the LORD said, "You pity the plant, for which you did not labor, nor did you make it grow, which came into being in a night, and perished in a night. And should not I pity Nineveh, that great city, in which there are more than a hundred and twenty thousand persons who do not know their right hand from their left, and also much cattle?"

Jonah—Provincial Prophet in a Jet Age

His name was Jonah Burke, but his close friends all called him Jon. As a wealthy industrialist, he was the owner of a firm on the West Coast known to be the beneficiary of lucrative defense contracts year after year. Jon Burke was proud of his patriotism, although he had no war record to boast of. During World War II he had been much too busy making huge profits manufacturing airplane parts. During the fifties, when he moved into missile component production the company which bore his name offered profit-anxious investors plenty of "guilt-edged" security.

Yet despite his absorbing business interests, Jon Burke was known as a man of God. He attended worship with the same regularity that he took his vitamins. He was a double-tither in his church, and had been a heavy contributor to their extensive building programs.

During the 1960's, in the name of God and country, he felt he had been called to organize a great crusade to save mankind. The slogan for the new movement was "Peace through triumph over Communism." Thousands joined the movement. Great throngs gathered in giant rallies under the crusade's banner. This gave Jon Burke an excellent opportunity to practice his outstanding oratorical ability. The core of his message was this: "Atheistic Communism is encroaching on our freedom everywhere in the world. We must expose this menace to a free and competitive society here at home and awaken our fellow Americans to the threat abroad. Above all, we must take the initiative—not just react to pressure but put Communism on the defensive." (He never quite spelled out what he meant by this, but it went over well with his enthusiastic audiences.) Though no lists of Jon Burke Society members were ever made public, it was rumored that the movement had hundreds of thousands, perhaps millions, of supporters.

As the movement grew, it was increasingly difficult to keep disreputable characters out, and undoubtedly a number of crackpots joined—this despite the unrelenting criticism by the Jon Burkers of Communist infiltration in the State Department, the AFL-CIO, the churches, etc.

THE VISION

Arriving home from a rally late one evening, Jon went to bed exhausted and fell into a dreamless sleep. In the middle of the night he felt himself stabbed suddenly awake. The room was dark, but he heard a voice call to him: "Jonah, Jonah!"

"Yes, Lord!" said Jon Burke, breaking out in a cast-iron sweat.

"Listen, you are to be my chosen servant to speak to my beloved children, the Russians."

"Your *be-beloved?*"

"Yes, like all mankind they are my beloved—though erring—children."

"Bu-but why me?"

"They need my message and you are able to give it to them."

"But they do not deserve salvation, and besides, they surely will never listen to me!"

But now the room was empty and silent—except for Jon's heavy breathing and the thumping of his heart. Contemplating the meaning of his experience, Jon Burke did not rest well the balance of the night. A less spiritual man might have ignored such an apparition, but the matter greatly troubled Jon Burke's thoughts.

The next day a strange-looking, well-postmarked piece of mail arrived at the Burke residence. It was from the Soviet Union and inside the letterhead read: MOSCOW PEACE CONGRESS. Jon found that he was invited to speak before that body early next summer. Burke had heard of this type of annual gathering before but had dismissed it as a lightly veiled attempt on the part of the Communists to influence and indoctrinate naïve representatives of neutral and Western Nations. The word "peace" in such instances served as enticing bait.

So plagued was Jon's conscience for the next few weeks that he could neither work nor sleep. The last place he wished to go was Moscow. The last thing he wanted to do was to deliver an address at the seat of the Kremlin. Had he not himself chastised those who associated with such evil-doers? Yet, there had been the vision and the invitation that immediately followed.

THE ESCAPE

Needing time to think the whole thing over, and perhaps put it out of his mind entirely, Jon decided on a spring vacation —a yachting trip to the Bermudas. He gathered a few business associates together, flew across country, and together they shoved off from Tampa Bay where he had stored one of his boats. He throttled down the coast and through the Keys and headed east.

Storm warnings had been sounded in the vicinity, but the weather was open and clear immediately ahead. At a leisurely thirty knots the *Patriot* eased by Cuba some twenty-five nautical miles to the north. Jon had cautioned his fellow crewmen against brushing too close to that "Devil's Island of the Caribbean" for fear of contamination.

When Cuba was a half-day's view behind, Jon sighted a crippled fishing vessel on the port side ahead. It was a small Russian trawler listing precariously. Apparently its communications equipment was out of order for there was no response to radio signals. But the *Patriot* crew could see the Russian seamen waving wildly upon the deck of the uptilted side. "We just can't let them sink, Russians or no Russians!" muttered Burke. He drew alongside the obviously doomed vessel, risking the peril of being sucked under should the trawler suddenly decide to sleep on the bed of the sea.

There were eight men aboard—all smelling of fish, but the *Patriot* made room for them—at considerable inconvenience to the crew of businessmen. Needless to say, piscatorial fragrance predominated over the pleasant perfume of lingering after-shave lotion.

Fortunately, one of the Russian fishermen had had some contact with Americans at the close of World War II and knew some simple English. Their ship had been hit by a sudden squall, he revealed. So great had been the impact of the waves that even the lifeboats had been broken up. They had headed toward Cuba but didn't quite make it.

The *Patriot* redirected its course toward Puerto Rico, the closest friendly port. Along the way Jon Burke and his friends were amazed to find how easily they fell into comradeship with these simple Russian sailors. It seemed somehow impossible that they were citizens of an "enemy" nation. *Patriot* crew members rather reluctantly relinquished their shipwrecked companions at San Juan. The Soviet fishermen were profuse in their thanksgiving, especially to Jon, who they said "saved their lives." Jon did not mind for he had acquired another story to tell which would point up the superiority of American-made vessels over Russian.

Burke and company refueled and pointed once more toward the beautiful Bermudas. Midway, they picked up on their radio serious warnings about new squall formations. Before they could decide on the best course, a storm hit their starboard side with such ferocity that it felt as though they had been swatted repeatedly by the hand of the devil. There was nothing to do but pray and ride it out. By the time the tempest subsided, the *Patriot* crew was almost afraid to survey the damage. No leak was discovered, but they were dismayed upon learning that the ship's rudder mechanism had been rendered inoperable.

All they could do was to issue an S.O.S. and hope they would not be left to drift for days. Fortunately, the following day an American nuclear-powered submarine surfaced beside them and the whole *Patriot* crew was taken aboard. They were informed by the captain that the sub was headed for London and that due to the pressure of time, they could not afford to put in at any other port. Thus, Jon Burke resigned himself to being confined in the belly of a Polaris sub for at least three days. Depressed, as he lay restlessly upon his bed that night, giving silent voice to his emotions, he prayed:

"O Lord, I call to thee *out of my distress,*
   believing that thou wilt be faithful to my supplications.

For though thou hast permitted me to suffer calamity,
  yet canst thou deliver me.
Thou hast laid thine hand upon me;
like the suit of a deep-sea diver
    have I felt weighed down by it.
Here am I, *the waters closed in over me,*
  the deep was round about me.
And yet though seaweed entangle me,
  it shall be to me the enfolding arms of thee.
If I take the wings of the morning
    and dwell in the uttermost parts of the sea,
  *even there thy hand shall lead me.**
Though my soul faints within me,
  thou art the same Lord, whose mercy is everlasting.
There are those who worship idols,
  who are more materialistic than Marxist ideology,
  who *forsake their true loyalty.*
But I, with the voice of thanksgiving,
  will sacrifice to thee.
Upon thy compelling altar
    I offer up my resistant spirit.
For at the last I know—
    Deliverance belongs to the Lord!"

Then after what seemed like many minutes, the Lord spoke
in Jon's inner ear:
"My servant, Jonah, do not fear.
  You shall be released to do my work.
Go now to the people of Moscow;
  do not be troubled over what to say:
I will put my words into your heart."

Then suddenly the room seemed very quiet, but the warm
glow lingered and the certainty of the future prevailed. That
night Jon Burke slept well.

When the sub heaved to the surface at London and let Jon off

* Psalm 139.

at that British capital city, he pulled out of his pocket the crumpled invitation he had received several weeks before and wired Moscow his belated acceptance.

THE SPEECH

Three days later, Jon found himself in comfortable quarters in the Leningrad Hotel of Moscow. He had contacted the conference officials, and they were delighted to have him speak at their gathering. It appeared to him that their profuse welcome revealed their belief that he would provide some much-needed window dressing. True, he was known as a "peace" speaker in the United States, but his usual point was that we must deal with the Russians from a "situation of strength" to bring them to terms agreeable to us. Also, we must "stand up to them" and "be firm."

At any rate, he could not understand why they had invited him. At least he felt safe in Moscow—it was the last place on earth the devil would look for him! Perhaps, as had so often happened in the States, his name had been confused with John Burt, the well-known American religious pacifist. If this were so, mused Jon, the intelligence network of the Communists was not as strong as he had often claimed in his public speeches.

In any event, he would give them a strong message they would not soon forget. He was sure they would not arrest him—his U. S. passport would protect him. He placed his hand in his right breast pocket to make sure it was still there. Also, as he thought over the prospect of his future address, he was sure this would not tarnish his image in America. In fact, it would probably brighten it up. In his own mind he was already working on a speech he would be able to deliver with the greatest enthusiasm back in the States; it was to be built around the biblical story "Daniel in the Lion's Den."

The Leningrad Hotel, where Jon stayed, was built in 1954 and was plush by Old World standards. However, he noticed that there were no stairways or fire escapes above the fourth floor. "What difference does it make," he thought. "This is where they house their foreign visitors—Americans, British, and the like!"

He also was well aware that the doorman picked up the telephone every time he walked in and out.

The first time he went to his room (on the fourth floor, fortunately!) he tried the key in the lock. It would slip in, but it wouldn't turn. At this point a hotel porter hurried up to him and in agitated Russian shouted at him: "No, not this room! That one!" He pointed to the room next door. Jon then took a close look at the obstinate door. It had a seal on it similar to those used to seal filled boxcars. Whoever had that room obviously didn't want anyone else going in without his knowledge. From that time on he suspected that his own room was bugged—with listening devices located in the adjacent quarters. After that experience he decided *not* to practice his talk orally in his room.

It was called to Jon Burke's attention that he was to speak at 3 P.M. on the second day. The Soviet premier spoke on the first day in a special session held in Red Square. Some 100,000 persons, in addition to the 2500 delegates, heard him. As he mounted the podium, he cleared his throat and spat in the general direction of Stalin's slab. Then he adjusted his spectacles, and in an impromptu manner delivered his prepared statement. His speech before the Peace Congress represented the traditional Soviet position. It centered around several main points:

"Peaceful coexistence . . . mutual renunciation of war as a means of settling disputes . . . no surrender to the forces of aggression . . . intrigues of imperialist warmongers . . . German peace treaty will be signed . . . support to peoples fighting to free themselves from imperialist and colonial oppression . . . business cooperation with all countries . . ." The Soviet leader was given the usual extended rousing ovation.

When Jon Burke returned to his hotel later that evening, he met an American newspaperman who had just flown in from Paris. He had the Paris edition of the New York *Herald Tribune* with him. A startling story commanded the whole front page of this otherwise staid publication. According to the account:

"A 100-megaton bomb accidentally exploded this morning in central Siberia . . . It is estimated that more than 50,000 persons were killed by the blast and deadly radiation in this underpopulated area of the world . . . Wind currents have carried radioactive fallout into northern China thus causing further tension in the Soviet-Chinese rift."

"How awful!" exclaimed Jon. "But it was bound to happen—somewhere." Amazing, he thought to himself, that the prime minister made no mention of the catastrophe. Jon went to his room and revised his speech somewhat, taking this latest development into account.

The next morning, as Jon strode through the streets of Moscow, he noticed that the people were in a very somber mood; they almost walked mechanically and seemed to be staring in the general direction of outer space. Fear and resentment were apparent in their countenances.

Jon visited the American Embassy to check on the details of the previous day's disaster. Yes, it was true, although the Soviet government sought to minimize the incident. They made a routine radio announcement of the matter that morning—buried in among reports on crop prospects. But the whole world knew the truth; seismic recording devices in Sweden first picked it up. American Air Force planes based in Japan were beginning to take samples of the atmosphere in order to make a thorough check.

"But why," said Jon, "did they not immediately blame it on American espionage, gain a propaganda advantage, and attempt to cloud the whole issue?"

The embassy official commented: "That might seem to offer the best explanation and would serve to gain sympathy from the neutrals and to whip up patriotic fervor at home. However, apparently the government feels that such a public interpretation would be too great an admission; it would inspire insecurity among the people and raise the ire of the military, who are already inclined toward committing a coup for security purposes. Besides, this gives Soviet leadership an excuse to clamp down on the top brass who are a constant threat to their position."

That afternoon Jon entered the Kremlin—which he discovered was just a group of government buildings with a red wall around them. He was utterly astounded and puzzled in observing that, within the very walls of the Kremlin, several Russian Orthodox churches were open with worshipers attending services therein. "What?" he asked himself, "Christians worshiping God in the very shadows of a government that teaches atheism?"

He sought out the huge convention hall the Peace Congress used for its headquarters. It was a large auditorium; 2500 delegates and, in addition, 3500 observers and visitors, mostly Russian, were seated. The time came for him to deliver his address. As the moment approached, he recalled that passage in the Scriptures: ". . . do not be anxious beforehand what you are to say; but say whatever is given you in that hour, for it is not you who speak, but the Holy Spirit."* Jon hazily heard his name mentioned in a routine introduction, and he rose to speak. It seemed to him that at that very moment the Holy Spirit took hold of him—he found himself saying things which he had not even intended to say. His message, in brief, was as follows:

"I wish to begin by expressing my deep grief upon hearing of the tragic accident which has befallen the Soviet people. I am sure that all American citizens join with me in mourning your loss and reflecting soberly upon the proper response to this most calamitous event.

"We, the peoples of the world, can tolerate no longer an arms race which promises death as the lone victor. You and I want our children and grandchildren to have the chance to grow up and to cherish the values we uphold. This will not be possible unless we decide that those things which bind us together as men are more important than those things which divide us as nations.

"The common people of the Soviet Union surely want peace. We are well aware of their agonizing suffering during World War II—with twenty million of their citizens perishing in the struggle. We Americans have not known such loss since the time of the Civil War when more than a half million, North and South, lost their lives. The American people, I can assure you, want peace also, with all their hearts.

"We realize that there is much misunderstanding between us. We were surprised at the violent Russian reaction to the U-2 incident. Perhaps we do not fully understand the natural resent-

* Mark 13:11.

ment of the Soviet Union occasioned by intrusion of her borders. For yours is a country which has known ill respect for boundaries —invaded at least once every century since A.D. 900. We Americans have suffered only one invasion of our continent in all our history—when the British occupied Washington and burned our Capitol during the War of 1812.

"Thus, we do not understand one another. And you do not realize the resentment we feel when Russian spies are discovered operating in the United States. Let us together work for a world where no man snoops on another, where no nation plots evil secretly against another, but *all* nations share their advantages and scientific developments for the blessing of all mankind.

"Why are we competing in a project called 'the race to the moon'? Both the Soviet Union and the United States are involved in multibillion-dollar expenditures each year to travel to the moon. Why? Will the moon sustain life? Probably not—or not very adequately. Will this make possible trips to other potentially inhabited planets? No. The planet Venus boils with 800-degree temperatures. Can we expect soon to visit the stars? Indeed not. The closest star in our galaxy is more than twenty trillion miles away. At present rocket speeds it would take thousands of years to get there.

"Why then are we involved in this madness? To prove to the other nations of the world that our particular way of life is superior. But are the nations of Asia and Africa especially impressed by these wasteful million-dollar shots into space—when so many of their people are living on the slenderest margin of existence for lack of basic necessities? Let us then compete peacefully, as your Premier has said. Let us postpone for the time being this escapist trip to the moon; instead let us use the ten billion dollars per year that our brethren around the world may have the tools to fashion a life of economic independence and humanitarian achievement! [At this, the delegates from Africa, Asia, and Latin America stood spontaneously and applauded.]

"Ever since World War II we have not taken the problem of disarmament very seriously. Each side has attempted to secure the disarmament of the other at the point of its greatest strength. There must be concessions—concessions which are made, not to the other side, but for the sake of a concern for the security of common humanity. This latter need was made all too apparent by the lamentable event of yesterday.

"The bomb dropped on Hiroshima was only a baby—20 kiloton—yet capable of extinguishing 100,000 lives. In the last decade this bomb was replaced by the standard weapon in the arsenals of the nuclear powers—the 20-megaton H-bomb—so powerful as to be the equivalent in fire power to all the bullets shot, shells fired, and bombs dropped in all of World War II by all participants! Now we have the 100-megaton weapon—and we have seen what it can do.

"Do we, whether Christian, Communist, Buddhist, or agnostic, have the moral restraint necessary to control all of this power in our own lifetime? Let us then return to the conference table again and again. There are risks no matter what we do. In a disarmament agreement the U.S. is risking the dangers involved in moving away from a defense-oriented economy. In a thorough inspection system the U.S.S.R. risks opening up its somewhat secret society.

"But as there are dangers of loss, there are also prospects for gain. Would life not be better if there were no longer a ring of bases around the Soviet Union? Would there not be much relief in the world if no country had cause to be anxious about Russian missile-armed submarines along the Atlantic coast or Polaris subs in the Mediterranean? Would not all countries feel safer if they could be assured that no missiles were pointed in their direction from bases near or far? Would not tensions be eased if there were no military secrets to be carefully guarded—thus rendering obsolete the role of the international spy?

"As a Christian, then, in the name of Christ, I beseech you to know the blessing of being "peacemakers," to call your own countries to a peace that is more than a slogan or an empty word. For true peace means:

—to work for those objectives which will serve the world's

need, unconcerned about buttressing our own nation's pride;
—to labor for all means of building trust and faith and confidence and to frown upon all policies that rouse suspicion;
—to promote understanding of the feelings of all other nations rather than to judge them harshly with partial truth;
—to be willing to take the risks now in a disarmament agreement lest tomorrow's world make probable our mutual annihilation.

"Today it is not the United States and the Soviet Union alone which face nuclear destruction. We are collectively threatened by a countdown on all humanity. Perhaps the count has already moved on down to ten or five. The question is: 'Will it hold there?' Can we be assured that the accident experienced yesterday will not be repeated? Or that, if such repetition occurred in any country, it would not be misinterpreted as a first-strike attack?

"Let us repent and move now into that world where swords are beat into plowshares, spears into pruning hooks, and atom bombs into useful sources of energy for the benefit of all mankind. *Spa-see-bah*."*

Jon Burke left the platform in somewhat of a daze. He felt as though he had just spoken in tongues. Not a page of the manuscript he brought with him had been turned. He recalled the silence and then what sounded to him like polite applause as he left the hall and headed back to his hotel room. He had a headache and could hardly remember anything of what he had said.

THE AFTERMATH

His plane was due out in two hours—so he had time only to pack and ride out to the Moscow airport. He had no customs problem because he had made no purchases—since he was thoroughly convinced that the Russians had nothing worth buying. He bypassed the syrupy-looking coffee available and instead spent a few kopeks for a glass of milk which helped him to gain a few hours of sleep on the airliner to East Berlin. As the airport bus rolled into West Berlin, the passengers let out a cheer, and Jon

* "Thank you" in Russian.

felt very much like squatting down and kissing the precious free soil.

Jon rose early from a good night's sleep and went to the lobby to purchase an English language newspaper. The headlines which captured his eyes seemed unbelievable: AMERICAN LAUNCHES PEACE BREAKTHROUGH! RUSSIANS SHOW CHANGE OF HEART. A two-column wire dispatch flanked by pictures told the story:

> Well-known American anti-Communist Jon Burke proved the catalytic agent which launched the greatest demonstration seen in Moscow since the days of the October Revolution in 1917.
>
> Burke, speaking passionately before a session of the Moscow Peace Congress, called for a halt to the arms race and the moon race. He challenged the Soviet Union to make new attempts at a disarmament agreement and to compete with the United States through a massive economic aid program. His address was delivered against the backdrop of the previous day's sobering event—the accidental explosion of a 100-megaton bomb in Siberia.
>
> The full impact of Mr. Burke's speech began to be felt late yesterday afternoon and evening as the news of its message swept rapidly through the capital city by word of mouth. Spontaneously crowds began to gather in Red Square until more than a million people had assembled in that area. The Muscovites were in a high emotional pitch which seemed to be motivated at once by fear, resentment, and desperate hope. They began to chant in unison: "Mir! Mir! Mir!"* So lusty were these resounding shouts it seemed that the adjacent Kremlin walls would come tumbling down. The people were extremely overwrought: men raised their fists; many women knelt to pray with tears running down their cheeks—the streetsweepers of Moscow never washed the streets as clean.
>
> After almost two hours of demonstrations, the prime min-

* "Peace."

ister walked from the Kremlin area and mounted the platform at the Lenin mausoleum. He publicly and informally promised the people two things: (1) the following day would be declared a national day of mourning; (2) the government would speedily take the practical steps necessary to reach a disarmament agreement with the United States.

The Kremlin subsequently released to the press the text of a telegram sent by the Soviet premier to the President of the United States. The text read as follows:
"My esteemed Mr. President:

In the light of the most tragic event of recent days and for the future welfare of humankind, the Soviet Union requests that disarmament negotiators reconvene immediately at Geneva. We are pleased to announce in advance that the U.S.S.R. will accept any reasonable inspection plan agreed upon by the unaligned states.

Premier of the U.S.S.R."

Impartial observers from the Western world were assessing this initiative as a typical Russian stroke of genius through which they may effectively bear the image of "Peacemaker" and at the same time appeal to the ego of neutral nations.

What Jon Burke read angered him. How could these Communist warmongers who are out to "bury us" sincerely want peace? Were they not demons damned by God? How dare they pretend to repent! His cheeks burned so hot with rage that the tears of bitterness dried before they could fall from his face.

He went to his room and wept. "And to think," he sobbed, "that I had something to do with all of this! God, forgive me!" Later that morning a group of reporters came to his room for an interview. They found him unshaven, red-eyed, somewhat incoherent. He sat on the edge of the bed clutching the newspaper in one hand and his Jon Burke Society card in the other. Great tears fell upon the membership card. All he could say was, "My God, what have I done!"

Even the most zealous of the reporters decided it was the wrong time for an interview and regretfully departed.

In the early afternoon Jon decided to go for a walk. The sky had darkened and a foggy drizzle turned pedestrians to plodding silhouettes. Jon moved destinationless through clouds of moisture which left dew drops on his bristled face. He was oblivious to all; but at one corner he stopped before the open door of a church. By the soft light that outlined the chancel he saw that the church was vacant. He went in—for it was not uncommon for him to turn to the church in the dark moments of his life.

At the chancel he prostrated himself before the altar and prayed fervently: "I beseech thee, O Lord, *is not this what I said when I was yet in my country*? I knew that it was wrong for me to undertake this mission. That is why I tried to get away from it all through the sea cruise. *For I knew that thou art a gracious God and merciful, slow to anger, and abounding in steadfast love . . . Therefore now, O Lord, take my life from me, I beseech thee, for it is better for me to die than to live.*"

He pressed his throbbing forehead against the cool marble communion rail for what seemed like a long time. Then he felt something quivering and wet at his side. Startled, he looked down to see a small nondescript dog which had wandered into the refuge of the sanctuary. The animal was shivering uncontrollably and was so wet that his clinging fur shrunk his body to grotesque proportions. "Poor thing," said Jon sympathetically, "I understand just how you feel." Almost instinctively Jon took out his clean handkerchief and began wiping the dog dry. When this proved insufficient, he took off his white silk scarf (for it was chilly that day) and began to use it as a towel.

But this temporary diversion was not enough for Jon to overcome his persistent state of emotional travail. With the befriended pup at his side, he turned once more to airing his grievance before God: "Lord, O Lord, what have I done! What will happen to my crusade now? How can we keep the people alerted to creeping Communism? What will happen to my defense business? I wish I were dead!"

Suddenly he felt the mysterious presence of some third Being.

In a voice strangely familiar but always surprising to him, he heard these words: "Jonah, Jonah—*Do you do well to be angry?*"

"Yes, Lord," said Jon, "I am *angry enough to die.*"

"Why, Jonah, why? Do you remember? You had mercy upon the Russian fishermen; you also had pity upon this poor mongrel, which is here tonight and wandering the streets tomorrow. Therefore, should I not have pity upon Moscow, *that great city, in which there are more than a hundred and twenty thousand* infants *who do not know their right hand from their left,* and also some dogs?"

IV | JEREMIAH

Jeremiah—His Times and Ours

Jeremiah, trained as a priest in the tradition of his family, was called as a young man to be "a prophet to the nations." Although he protested, "I am only a youth," he was assured of the Lord's sustaining strength.

It was a difficult time in which to preach. Under the influence of Judah's King Manasseh (687-642 B.C.), who was an Assyrian puppet, religious decadence had set in. The temple had been closed; there was no formal worship of Yahweh.

The prophet proclaimed that Judah had deserted Yahweh, "the fountain of living waters." The nation had turned to false gods which were like broken cisterns, unable to hold water. Jeremiah had searched the streets of Jerusalem in vain to find even one man "who does justice and seeks truth" so that Judah might lay claim to pardon.

In 626 B.C., the year of Jeremiah's call, King Josiah came to power. Under the leadership of the good king, the temple at Jerusalem was repaired in 622 B.C. While this rebuilding project was in progress, the workmen chanced upon a scroll hidden in the walls. The document set forth specific laws by which the nation was expected to live. Basing their action on those laws, the king and his princes immediately launched a reform movement which forbade the worship of any other gods but Yahweh. All worship was to be restricted henceforth to the temple at Jerusalem. Justice was required in all human relationships.

It soon became clear, however, that the reform largely took the direction of nationalism, and Jeremiah was keenly disappointed. The changes which were initiated, instead of purging the soul of the nation, were largely superficial. Although the altars and pillars erected to pagan gods on every high hill were destroyed and temple ritual was now rigorously observed, there was no fundamental improvement in the life of the people. To make matters worse, the religious leaders supporting the movement saw nothing wrong.

Jeremiah was deeply disturbed by this hypocrisy. Judah had not returned to Yahweh "with her whole heart, but in pretense" (3:10). The prophet now saw that the people had in effect simply adopted a more respectable idolatry, placing their trust not in the Lord but in the ritual of the Jerusalem temple.

King Josiah died in 609 B.C. Now all restraint was removed from the nationalistic party which favored centralizing political and religious power in Jerusalem. Paying little attention to adverse economic conditions in Judah, the new king, Jehoiakim, decided to erect a lavish palace for his enjoyment. Built with forced labor, it was to be paneled with cedar and painted with vermilion. Learning of this, Jeremiah could not keep silent. "Do you think you are a king because you compete in cedar?" he asked.

About this time Jeremiah delivered his famous temple address (chapter 7) in which he denounced the hypocrisy he saw in temple worship. To the outraged priests and prophets he cried, "Will you steal, murder, commit adultery, swear falsely, burn incense to Baal, and go after other gods that you have not known, and then come and stand before me in this house, which is called by my name, and say, 'We are delivered!' " (7:9-10).

The religious leaders were furious, especially when he referred to the temple as a "den of robbers." Had it not been for support from some of the princes, Jeremiah might have been martyred for these pithy words of truth.

During the entire eleven years of Jehoiakim's reign, there was no letup in Jeremiah's criticisms. He persistently predicted destruction for a nation and people so given to folly. Barred from speaking publicly in the temple, Jeremiah dictated his oracles to his disciple, Baruch, who proceeded to read them in the courts of the sanctuary. On one occasion friends of Jeremiah arranged to have his scroll read before the king, who was sitting in his winter palace with a brazier burning beside him. As every three or four columns of the scroll were read, so irritated was the king that he would cut these off with a penknife and burn them in the fire, until finally the whole scroll was consumed.

When Jeremiah heard of this, he immediately dictated the words again to Baruch on another scroll and for good measure "there were added thereto many similar words"! The prophet would not allow book-burning to silence him.

After the death of Jehoiakim in 598 B.C., his son Jehoiachin ascended to the throne. Within a fateful three months, following a siege of Jerusalem, he was forced to surrender to the Babylonians. Thus Jehoiachin was taken to Babylon in captivity along with thousands of other members of the aristocracy. The Babylonians appointed his weak-kneed uncle, Zedekiah, as king in his place. With this turn of events, Jeremiah envisioned a new day eventually for the exiles who were suffering under the judgment of God, but he saw little future for the unrepentant people remaining in Judah. Although the prophets who accompanied the exiles to Babylon were encouraging them to look forward to a speedy return, Jeremiah denounced such optimism and suggested that the exiles make plans to remain in Babylon for many years.

Meanwhile, in violation of an oath of allegiance to Babylonia, in 593 B.C. Zedekiah joined in a plot with Edom, Moab, Ammon, Tyre, and Sidon to throw off Judah's new masters. Seeing no hope for his nation in its spiritual condition, Jeremiah counseled surrender when Zedekiah's revolt inspired a Babylonian army to march on Judah. For such traitorous advice, Pashur, an officer of the temple, had Jeremiah beaten and placed in stocks. Even the princes deserted him now. Once he was left to rot in the bottom of a slimy cistern. Through the intercession of the vacillating Zedekiah, Jeremiah was rescued, only to repeat his advice to the king that he should surrender to Babylon to spare his life and save the city.

After a long and bitter siege the city did indeed fall; its walls and temple were destroyed, Zedekiah was captured, and his sons were killed before his very eyes. Then he was blinded and carried off to Babylon in chains together with other members of the aristocracy.

Nebuchadrezzar, king of Babylon, offered Jeremiah the choice of either going to Babylon and receiving favored treatment or remaining behind with the remnant of the people. Jeremiah was not unpatriotic, as his accusers often suggested; he stayed behind and helped the newly appointed governor, Gedaliah, to rebuild the life of the people of Judah. Unfortunately his friend Gedaliah was murdered soon thereafter. Some of the princes involved in the plot fled to avoid punishment by the Babylonians, taking Jeremiah with them to Egypt. There he continued his task of prophesying, sending his oracles to the exiled community.

THE MAJOR TEACHINGS OF JEREMIAH

Jeremiah has been called "the father of true prayer." Until the time of Jeremiah, prayer had been largely petition. But Jeremiah's prayers were often "confessions," intimate conversations with God.

From Jeremiah we learn that *in personal prayer a man can bring before God any deep concern on his heart.* Thus he shared with God his anguish, his reproach, his hostility, his doubts, and his anxieties. Always he believed that God would understand and strengthen and guide him.

Another striking feature of Jeremiah's ministry was *his denunciation of all deceit and hypocrisy.* Jeremiah was particularly disgusted with the false prophets who spoke only what the people wanted to hear. They were fond of publicly proclaiming, "You shall not see the sword, nor shall you have famine, but I will give you assured peace in this place" (14:13). This kind of pronouncement Jeremiah classified as "a lying vision, worthless divination, and the deceit of their own minds" (14:14).

In his temple sermon Jeremiah made it abundantly clear that the temple worship would not succeed in saving the people of Judah. They were doomed if they persisted in following minutely the ritualistic prescriptions of Deuteronomy but neglected the weightier matters of the law—such as executing justice and having compassion upon the alien, the orphan, and the widow.

Jeremiah had yet another message of great importance. *God's law was to be written in people's hearts.* He had been so terribly disappointed in the outcome of the covenant relationship which had centered in the book of Deuteronomy. Although its code of laws had provided the impetus for the reform movement, it had become an object of worship itself, so that the citizens of Judah began to think of themselves as "the people of the book." The prescription "You shall bind them as a sign upon your hand" and "write them on the doorposts of your house" (Deut. 6:8, 9) became formalized by interpreters. Thus the people wore phylacteries on their foreheads and arms and placed mezuzahs on their doorposts. These containers with Scripture verses inside them seemed to falsely assure their users that they would be free of all danger.

The covenant with the nation had not succeeded in redeeming the people. So Jeremiah said the Lord would make a new covenant with the house of Israel. "I will put my law within them, and I will write it upon their hearts; and I will be their God, and they shall be my people. And no longer shall each man teach his neighbor and each his brother, saying, 'Know the LORD,' for they shall all know me, from the least of them to the greatest, says the LORD; for I will forgive their iniquity, and I will remember their sin no more" (31:33-34).

Fortified by this belief, men no longer needed the Ark, the Torah, or the temple to assure them of God's abiding presence; he had written his law in their hearts. With such a covenant men could be holy in Babylon as well as in Judah.

JEREMIAH'S MESSAGE FOR THE MODERN ERA

If Jeremiah were alive today he would stress *our need for greater depth in our prayer life*. The average Christian layman today prays in church when the clergyman leads, occasionally repeats the Lord's Prayer, and joins in spirit when his children say "God is gracious, God is good" at the table. Otherwise, largely because of the pressure of time, he does not commune with God.

Though no one lived a more hectic life than Jeremiah, yet he found time to pray. When we hold conversations with God, we need to take a cue from the praying prophet and wait for God to speak to us. When Jeremiah asked God difficult questions, he

allowed time for God to answer. Personal prayer is two-way traffic. A part of every devotional period should be set aside for listening.

If we decide to take the time we think we cannot spare, it will
mean much to us in terms of less anxiety, greater serenity, and
more assurance with respect to our direction in life.

A second valid truth Jeremiah would bring to our generation
is *our need for the law to be written in our hearts*. Like the
ancient Hebrews we tend to think that the externalization of our
religion will save us, that what we need is a new revision of the
Scriptures to reform the people, a new book of worship, a new
hymnal, or a new national shrine. These instruments, properly
used, can help. But our experience could also be the same as that
of the people after Josiah's reform—the deification of the trap-
pings of religion to the detriment of the heart of religion.

Jeremiah in his lifetime had witnessed the possibilities to be
found in God's making of a covenant that centered in a nation
and a church. The results were far from satisfying. Now God
would write the law upon their hearts. It was to be a "natural law"
woven within the very fabric of human nature, not some external
body of rules.

Jeremiah was saying that the individual does not depend for
his salvation on being related to some particular nation favored
by God. Nor does he depend upon the special grace of being included within the framework of some spiritual community. *He
stands alone before God.* Yet he is not helpless, for God has
chosen to write his laws upon men's hearts. "They shall all know
me . . . for I will forgive their iniquity," says the Lord (31:34).
In other words, men will be aware of God working in their hearts
as they recognize his merciful forgiveness. It is then this mercy, this
grace, which leads a man *naturally* to follow the law from his
heart.

When one recognizes this embryonic truth in Jeremiah's
teaching more than 2500 years ago, it is a great mystery as to why
it is so long in taking hold upon us. For Paul clearly taught:
"You are not under law but under grace" (Rom. 6:14). Martin
Luther stressed justification by faith through grace. And it was

John Wesley's emphasis upon the mercy and undeserved love of God that caused tears of repentance to run down the cheeks of hard-bitten British miners.

At the home of Simon the Pharisee, when a sinful woman anointed his feet with precious ointment, Jesus said: "He who is forgiven little, loves little" (Luke 7:47). He implied that "He who is forgiven much loves much." *Forgiveness creates repentance* and moves the forgiven person to works of love.[1]

A further word of counsel in keeping with Jeremiah's emphasis would be: *Americans need to overcome their false sense of security and seek the kind of peace which will offer more hope for true security.*

Jeremiah was greatly disturbed as he saw his nation following a course of action which would inevitably lead her to utter annihilation. "My anguish, my anguish! I writhe in pain! Oh, the walls of my heart! My heart is beating wildly; I cannot keep silent; for I hear the sound of the trumpet, the alarm of war" (4:19).

But no one seemed to care. The people thought they were safe in their multiple alliances, and Judah continued to follow those policies which would assure her destruction by powerful Babylonia. The situation for the United States is quite different today with respect to her power relationship to the Soviet Union. While tiny Judah, with or without alliances, could not rationally hope for more than a subservient relationship to mighty Babylon, the United States has undoubtedly greater strength than the U.S.S.R. Even so, because of the nuclear dilemma, an atomic war with Russia today would bring the United States to a worse disaster than Jeremiah contemplated for war-bent Judah.

We also tend to be cursed by the same misplaced confidence in our security that centuries ago worked against the best interests of Judah. We rest our safety in fallout shelters and overkill capacity. Admittedly, fallout shelters will not protect our cities, where most of our people live, because the destruction wrought by blast and firestorm nullify any protection such shelters might otherwise provide.

Despite the United States' overkill capacity advantage in relation to the Soviet Union, we are not certain of our ability to adequately defend our own population and territory. The United States has an overkill of 1250 in relation to the U.S.S.R.'s overkill of 290.[2] An overkill of one means the capacity, through the use of deliverable nuclear power, to utterly destroy all major population centers in the land of the enemy twice. This means that the Soviet Union today, with less overkill capacity, would be able to utterly destroy the United States in a nuclear war even if 99 per cent of her missiles and bombers were shot down. A 99 per cent defense capability is, of course, unheard of. Thus, we are in the irrational position of continuing to stockpile overkill even though it adds nothing to our ability to defend ourselves. We are victims of a misplaced confidence that our arms buildup provides additional security when in reality it does not.

Such a false sense of security can be likened to the attitude that preceded the sinking of the *Titanic*. The ship was believed to be unsinkable. But it went down, and the thing that "couldn't happen" happened.

Today it would be a fatal mistake to be lulled into a false sense of security by a growing stockpile of H-bombs or a profusion of civil defense signs at shelters which may protect against fallout but not against fall-in.

Instead, for true security we should seek safeguarded, worldwide, and complete disarmament. There are those who feel that such an agreement with the Soviet Union is impossible. But, as John J. McCloy, a U.S. negotiator on disarmament, points out, a century and a half ago the relationships of the United States with Canada were just as strained as are those between our country and the U.S.S.R. today.

During the War of 1812 the Canadians had burned Washington, D.C. Forts bristled prominently at the U.S.-Canadian border and occasionally blood was spilled. Despite the mounting tension and over the objections of military leadership of both nations, each side agreed to limit the number of warships on the Great Lakes. Soon after this the forts fell into disuse, and in time relationships so improved that no arms were needed along the border at all.[3] An effective disarmament agreement between Russia and the United States could open up the way for a similar modus vivendi between East and West.

We can be sure that Jeremiah would agree today with this advice from the New Testament:

"... seek peace and pursue it;
For the eyes of the Lord are upon the righteous,
and his ears are open to their prayer...."

(1 Peter 3:11-12.)

Selections from Jeremiah

THE CALL OF JEREMIAH   1:4-10

Now the word of the LORD came to me saying,
  "Before I formed you in the womb I knew you,
  and before you were born I consecrated you;
  I appointed you a prophet to the nations."
  Then I said, "Ah, Lord GOD! Behold, I do not know how to
speak, for I am only a youth." But the LORD said to me,
  "Do not say, 'I am only a youth';
  for to all to whom I send you you shall go,
  and whatever I command you you shall speak.
  Be not afraid of them,
  for I am with you to deliver you,

                                        says the LORD."
  Then the LORD put forth his hand and touched my mouth;
and the LORD said to me,
  "Behold, I have put my words in your mouth.
  See, I have set you this day over nations and over kingdoms,
  to pluck up and to break down,
  to destroy and to overthrow,
  to build and to plant."

THE APOSTASY OF ISRAEL   2:1-8, 11-13

  The word of the LORD came to me, saying, "Go and proclaim
in the hearing of Jerusalem, Thus says the LORD,
  I remember the devotion of your youth,
    your love as a bride,
  how you followed me in the wilderness,
    in a land not sown.
  Israel was holy to the LORD,
    the first fruits of his harvest.

All who ate of it became guilty;
  evil came upon them,

                                                says the LORD."

Hear the word of the LORD, O house of Jacob, and all the
families of the house of Israel. Thus says the LORD:
  "What wrong did your fathers find in me
    that they went far from me,
  and went after worthlessness, and became worthless?
  They did not say, 'Where is the LORD
    who brought us up from the land of Egypt,
  who led us in the wilderness,
    in a land of deserts and pits,
  in a land of drought and deep darkness,
    in a land that none passes through,
    where no man dwells?'
  And I brought you into a plentiful land
    to enjoy its fruits and its good things.
  But when you came in you defiled my land,
    and made my heritage an abomination.
  The priests did not say, 'Where is the LORD?'
    Those who handle the law did not know me;
  the rulers transgressed against me;
    the prophets prophesied by Baal,
    and went after things that do not profit. . . .
  Has a nation changed its gods,
    even though they are no gods?
  But my people have changed their glory
    for that which does not profit.
  Be appalled, O heavens, at this,
    be shocked, be utterly desolate,

                                        says the LORD,

  for my people have committed two evils:
    they have forsaken me,
  the fountain of living waters,
    and hewed out cisterns for themselves,
  broken cisterns,
    that can hold no water."

THE POWERLESS GODS 2:26-28

"As a thief is shamed when caught,
  so the house of Israel shall be shamed:
they, their kings, their princes,
  their priests, and their prophets,
who say to a tree, 'You are my father,'
  and to a stone, 'You gave me birth.'
For they have turned their back to me,
  and not their face.
But in the time of their trouble they say,
  'Arise and save us!'
But where are your gods
  that you made for yourself?
Let them arise, if they can save you,
  in your time of trouble . . ."

MERCY FOR A FAITHLESS ISRAEL 3:12-13

Return, faithless Israel,

                                          says the LORD.

I will not look on you in anger,
  for I am merciful,

                                          says the LORD;

I will not be angry for ever.
Only acknowledge your guilt,
  that you rebelled against the LORD your God
and scattered your favors among strangers under every green
  tree,
  and that you have not obeyed my voice,

                                          says the LORD.

FOLLY LEADS TO DISASTER 4:18-22

Your ways and your doings
  have brought this upon you.
This is your doom, and it is bitter;
  it has reached your very heart.

My anguish, my anguish! I writhe in pain!
  Oh, the walls of my heart!
My heart is beating wildly;
  I cannot keep silent;
for I hear the sound of the trumpet,
  the alarm of war.
Disaster follows hard on disaster,
  the whole land is laid waste.
Suddenly my tents are destroyed,
  my curtains in a moment.
How long must I see the standard,
  and hear the sound of the trumpet?
"For my people are foolish,
  they know me not;
they are stupid children,
  they have no understanding.
They are skilled in doing evil,
  but how to do good they know not."

THE NATION ENJOYS FALSE PROPHECY 5:21, 26-31

"Hear this, O foolish and senseless people,
  who have eyes, but see not,
  who have ears, but hear not. . . .
For wicked men are found among my people;
  they lurk like fowlers lying in wait.
They set a trap;
  they catch men.
Like a basket full of birds,
  their houses are full of treachery;
therefore they have become great and rich,
  they have grown fat and sleek.
They know no bounds in deeds of wickedness;
  they judge not with justice
the cause of the fatherless, to make it prosper,
  and they do not defend the rights of the needy.
Shall I not punish them for these things?
                  says the LORD,

and shall I not avenge myself
on a nation such as this?"
An appalling and horrible thing
has happened in the land:
the prophets prophesy falsely,
and the priests rule at their direction;
my people love to have it so,
but what will you do when the end comes?

A SINFUL PEOPLE WITHOUT SHAME 6:13-15

"For from the least to the greatest of them,
every one is greedy for unjust gain;
and from prophet to priest,
every one deals falsely.
They have healed the wound of my people lightly,
saying, 'Peace, peace,'
when there is no peace.
Were they ashamed when they committed abomination?
No, they were not at all ashamed;
they did not know how to blush.
Therefore they shall fall among those who fall;
at the time that I punish them, they shall be overthrown,"
says the LORD.

A PEOPLE POSSESSED BY EVIL 13:23-26

Can the Ethiopian change his skin
or the leopard his spots?
Then also you can do good
who are accustomed to do evil.
I will scatter you like chaff
driven by the wind from the desert.
This is your lot,
the portion I have measured out to you, says the LORD,
Because you have forgotten me
and trusted in lies.
I myself will lift up your skirts over your face,
and your shame will be seen.

DECEIT OF THEIR OWN MINDS   14:13-16

Then I said: "Ah, Lord GOD, behold, the prophets say to them, 'You shall not see the sword, nor shall you have famine, but I will give you assured peace in this place.' " And the LORD said to me: "The prophets are prophesying lies in my name; I did not send them, nor did I command them or speak to them. They are prophesying to you a lying vision, worthless divination, and the deceit of their own minds. Therefore thus says the LORD concerning the prophets who prophesy in my name although I did not send them, and who say, 'Sword and famine shall not come on this land': By sword and famine those prophets shall be consumed. And the people to whom they prophesy shall be cast out in the streets of Jerusalem, victims of famine and sword, with none to bury them—them, their wives, their sons, and their daughters. For I will pour out their wickedness upon them."

GOD WEARY OF RELENTING   15:5-7

"Who will have pity on you, O Jerusalem,
    or who will bemoan you?
Who will turn aside
    to ask about your welfare?
You have rejected me, says the LORD,
    you keep going backward;
so I have stretched out my hand against you and destroyed
        you;—
    I am weary of relenting.
I have winnowed them with a winnowing fork
    in the gates of the land;
I have bereaved them, I have destroyed my people;
    they did not turn from their ways.

LONELINESS OF THE TRUE PROPHET   15:15-18

O LORD, thou knowest;
    remember me and visit me,
    and take vengeance for me on my persecutors.
In thy forbearance take me not away;
    know that for thy sake I bear reproach.

Thy words were found, and I ate them,
  and thy words became to me a joy
  and the delight of my heart;
for I am called by thy name,
  O LORD, God of hosts.
I did not sit in the company of merrymakers,
  nor did I rejoice;
I sat alone, because thy hand was upon me,
  for thou hadst filled me with indignation.
Why is my pain unceasing,
  my wound incurable,
  refusing to be healed?
Wilt thou be to me like a deceitful brook,
  like waters that fail?

THE LORD SEARCHES THE HEART   17:9-11

The heart is deceitful above all things,
  and desperately corrupt;
  who can understand it?
"I the LORD search the mind
  and try the heart,
to give to every man according to his ways,
  according to the fruit of his doings."
Like the partridge that gathers a brood which she did not hatch,
  so is he who gets riches but not by right;
in the midst of his days they will leave him,
  and at his end he will be a fool.

Jeremiah—Spiritual Counselor for an Age of Anxiety

SPEAK FORTH THE TRUTH (1:6, 9, 17)

> *"Ah, Lord God! I do not know how to speak, for I am only a*
> *youth."*
> Do not despise your youth.
> They will not listen to you because of your age,
>   but because of what you have to say.
> I promise you, I shall *put my words in your mouth.*
> *Gird up your loins; arise, and say to them everything*
>   *that I command you.*
> *Do not be dismayed by them, lest I dismay you before them.*
> Speak forth the truth.
> Do not fear criticism should you touch a tender spot.
> Fear only the weakness in your knees,
>   and the quaver of your voice,
>   if tempted to speak in your own name.
> Know that I am with you, and that your voice is to be my Voice,
>   the words that you utter my Word.

THE PROMISED LAND (2:1-11)

> *The word of the Lord came to me, saying,*
> *Go and proclaim in the hearing of* Washington,
> *Thus says the Lord,*
> *I remember the devotion of your youth,*
> *your love as a bride,*
> *how you followed me in the wilderness,*
>   *in a land not sown.*
> America was holy to the Lord,
>   her pilgrims seeking a land of promise,
>   as did the ancient Israelites.

They came seeking the full richness of religious expression,
more treasured by them than fine gold.

What wrong did your fathers find in me,
that they went far from me,
and went after worthlessness,
and became worthless?

Have I been an indulgent Father, bestowing gifts upon you
more generously than you could appreciate?

When you came into this land of thick forest and rushing
stream,
fertile valley and verdant hill,
you were responsive to my grace.

As the generations passed, and wealth piled on wealth,
did you not begin to think, like a pampered child,
that the bounty you received was no more than you deserved?

And so, instead of thanking me, you thanked your common
sense,
your economic system, and your Yankee ingenuity.

When you came in you defiled my land.

You stripped my forests and consumed my ore;
you allowed a foot of topsoil to wash into the sea.

Are you proud to leave your grandchildren
such an inheritance—
deeds to farm land of rock and clay,
stock in a worn-out mine,
cash backed by an empty vault at Fort Knox?

Has a nation changed its gods,
even though they are no gods?
But my people have changed their glory
for that which does not profit.

BROKEN CISTERNS   (2:13)

For my people have committed two evils:
they have forsaken me, the fountain of living waters,
and hewed out cisterns for themselves,
broken cisterns, that can hold no water.

1000 pari-mutuel stubs—broken cisterns;

100 stock certificates that have lost their gilt edges—broken
    cisterns;
100 golf balls lost on the Sabbath—broken cisterns;
    a dozen well-worn personal credit cards—broken cisterns;
a 40-year mortgage on a 30-year house—broken cisterns;
    5,000,000 prospects for Alcoholics Anonymous—
      broken cisterns.

THE HARLOT'S BROW   (2:22; 3:3)

Though you wash yourself with lye and use much soap,
    the stain of your guilt is still before me.
About the dropping of the Hiroshima bomb,
    your whole society bears a guilt complex.
You are like the pilot who gave weather clearance for the drop,
    and later became mentally ill,
for you suffer from a national neurosis,
    knowing what you would blot out of your mind:
that on the morning of August 7, in the year 1945,
    the order was given to drop the bomb
    in the heart of a defenseless city,
    and it fell on a Buddhist temple in a park;*
that the order read "8:15 A.M."
    Why 8:15 in the morning?
    Because that was the optimum time:
      the men would be going to factories,
      the women going to market,
      the children going to school.
Outwardly *you have a harlot's brow,*
    you refuse to be ashamed.
Don your sackcloth and ashes!
Repent, or you will be unhappy
    until judgment satisfies your guilt.
Commit the works of repentance.
    Return the bomb to Pandora's box.

* See detailed map of Hiroshima prepared under direction of the Chief of Engineers
by the Army Map Service, 1945. This map shows completely destroyed and partially
destroyed sections of bombed area. Available in Map Reading Room, Library of
Congress.

TAILOR-MADE GODS   (2:27)

So America will be shamed when its priests and prophets,
  its statesmen and scientists,
say to the atom bomb:
  "You are my father,"
or to a stock certificate,
  "You gave me birth."
But from their foxholes they cry:
  "Arise and save us!"
And from the fallout shelters where they crouch, they plead:
  "Remember, God, this isn't a blast shelter!"
Where are your tailor-made gods then?

VICTIMS OF CLANDESTINE COUNCIL   (2:36, 37; 3:12, 13)

You shall be put to shame by others
        as you were at the Bay of Pigs,
*for the Lord has rejected those in whom you trust,
  and you will not prosper by them.*
Your military leaders have been overmilitant,
  your intelligence unintelligent:
    "An invasion of a few hundred Cubans can serve as a
catalytic agent for a successful counter-revolution."
    "The Russians are way ahead of us in missile production."
    "The advantages of U-2 overflights far outweigh any
risks to successful diplomacy."
    "We should not overlook the possibilities of becoming
a first-strike nation."
    "The Russians have an active Civil Defense program."
When will you act reasonably on facts open to all,
  instead of irrationally on secret dope,
  dope strong enough to dull both conscience and mind.
I will not be angry forever.
Only acknowledge your guilt,
  that you have sought clandestine counsel afar,
  and overlooked my guidance at hand.

DECEIVERS OF THE PEOPLE (4:9, 10)

In that day courage shall fail both premier and president; the politicians shall be appalled, and the men of the pulpit full of unbelief. Your scientists shall now have their unparalleled opportunity to make something out of nothing, to play Creator. In that day the Lord will say: "Where are those now who *utterly deceived this people,* saying radiation is as harmless as living in a brick house—the house that has fallen in on you! Where are those who said "97 per cent can be saved"? Are they among the 3 per cent who remain, only to die in three months?

Where are those who relied on "massive retaliation," strike-first strategy, hardened missile sites, impregnable defense, and "counter-force theory"? Do they have any force left with which to counter, any missiles with which to retaliate, any radar with which to review their own ruins?

SKILLED IN DOING EVIL (4:19-22)

My anguish; my anguish! I writhe in pain!
  Oh, the walls of my heart!
My heart is beating wildly;
  I cannot keep silent.
For my people do the stupid thing;
  they are naïve children.
They have no true understanding.
They are skilled in doing evil,
  but how to do good they know not.
Carnivals condition children to look on gambling with favor,
  identifying games of chance
  with ferris wheels and taffy apples.
Fathers teach sons how to drink like gentlemen.
Sergeants teach privates how to kill a man 21 ways.
TV teaches youngsters how to use chains to bruise,
  and hands to strangle.
From the school of experience they are taught
  all that the classroom denies.

Yet I would gather you up in my arms like a sleeping child;
  comfort you as a baby with colic,
  sit with you till your fever breaks,
  stand up for you in juvenile court,
  visit you in your death cell,
  mourn alone at your unmarked grave.

FOLLY OF CIVIL DEFENSE (5:21; 4:18)

Thus says the Lord:
  Hear this, O foolish and senseless people,
    who have eyes, but see not,
    who have ears, but hear not.
  I see a day of utter devastation
    for those who trusted in their own defense
    and not in the doing of my will.
  I made them human;
    they lived as subhuman.
  I made them creatures to walk on the face of the earth;
    they preferred to live beneath the earth.
  They added their shelters to their homes
    and neglected shelter for my homeless children.
  Shelters built for their security
    became for them a crematory.
  Their government began modestly with a 100-million-dollar
        program,
    but the unprotected demanded "protection."
  What began as a moderate expenditure escalated to a
        200-billion-dollar figure.
  Everything else had to wait:
    schools not built despite rising enrollments,
    roads crumbling away notwithstanding more traffic.
  Then the final battle was joined . . .
    it was over in five minutes.
  The innocent perished with the guilty.
  Neither democracy nor Communism won . . .
    only death.
  Missiles were launched from circling satellites.

Every corner became a scramble corner
  with no time to sound warning bells.
A few reached their "shelters";
  some not preferring burning to burial were awarded both.
The few survivors stayed in their shelters during the
      extended crisis period.
As a mushroom cloud rose slowly in the sky,
  men lived like cultured mushrooms
  crowded in the dark recesses of the earth.
I saw a man frantically operating an air pump,
  one approved by CD officials;
with every crank of the pump, he sucked in radioactive dust.
I saw another opening the flue to the "fresh air" above ground;
the 2000-degree surface temperatures drew into their holocaust
  what little oxygen remained in the shelter.

Such shall be the plight of a generation
  that refined its warning signals,
  but turned off the voice of God.
Despite severe hardships, a small minority did survive.
To what kind of world did they emerge?
  an earth crawling with spiders and bugs unharmed by
      radiation;
  a sky swarming with flies, feeding on the stinking
      carcasses of men and beasts,
  devoid of birds to devour locusts and winged insects;
  forests denuded by raging firestorms;
  streams polluted with Iodine 131 and all manner of dead
      things.
Did they rebuild?
O man, have you ever been able to make something out of
      nothing?
Your ways and your doings have brought this upon you,
  this is your doom, and it is bitter.
For you relied on a Civil Defense neither civilized
  nor capable of defending.

THE HAPPY CLOUDS

I see a world where children are playing in the park,
    where all the clouds in the sky are happy clouds,
where mushrooms are something found in steak sauce,
    and missiles transport life, not death.

PREACHING THE COMFORTABLE GOSPEL   (5:31)

The prophets prophesy falsely.
My people love to have it so,
    but what will you do when the end comes?
You make your descent seem so gradual and pleasant,
    like a non-swimmer easing himself into water over his head.
    Pity you, who preach to the rich!
How tempting it is, in your wealthy congregations,
    to preach a sermon intended
    to float merrily along on a sea of mink.
Is the mink so soft as to soften your speech?
Are there no "hard sayings" of Jesus in your pulpit gospel?
Do you speak of sharing Christ's sufferings?
    of making your bodies a living sacrifice?
    of seeking first the Kingdom of God?
    of loving one's enemies?
Or have you sold out to the mink?
Do you keep changing the sermon titles on your bulletin
       boards,
    but still preach on the same comfortable subjects:
    "Possessing Peace of Mind,"
    "Overcoming Your Troubles," or
       "How to Be Successful"?
Gird up your loins! Put on the whole armor of God!
Peruse the Scriptures! Preach on what needs to be heard!
Perspire and inspire!

LUST FOR UNJUST GAIN   (6:13, 14)

From the least to the greatest of them,
    every one is greedy for unjust gain.

Bored housewives play the stock market
  as though it were roulette at Las Vegas.
Cotton merchants invest in storage tanks
  nonexistent except for securing mortgages.
Sexagenarians put in their six quarters,
  to hit the Social Security jackpot.
Capitol Hill staff pulls strings for capital gain
Preachers and priests *have healed the wound of my people
    lightly,*
  saying "Have peace, have peace," when raging war threatens.

THE BODY OF CHRIST—A BASKET CASE

Thus says the Lord:
O you Christians, strength of my arm, voice of my mouth,
  compassion of my heart,
Step off your merry-go-round!
Break through your monotonous cycle!
  You who raise money to erect buildings,
  so you can expand your program,
and when you expand your program,
  you need more money to erect more buildings.
O when will you start *being* the church;
stop making the church a place to go to,
  and make it something to be;
stop building churches,
  and start being the Kingdom of God in the midst?
Stop making a basket case out of the Body of Christ!
Instead, make his Body active, virile, and whole,
with hands outstretched in service,
  feet swift to do my bidding,
  eyes quick to see the world's need,
  ears open to hear your brother's cry for help.

VISION OF THE FLOATING TOWER OF BABEL

I had a vision, a horrible vision,
  of a floating tower of Babel.

But it was not called Babel (though full of foreign tongues);
   it was called Lakonia.
The ship caught fire and sank into the sea—
   British passengers caught in confusion of orders issued by
      Greek and German crew,
   commands shouted in languages not understood—
   a disaster situation, with no communication.
"Too bad," says John Q. Citizen,
   turning to comics and sports page,
without comprehending that he, too, is on a ship,
   and the ship is burning.
No one mans the lifeboats,
   because they cannot converse and transmit meanings.
The blocs do not agree
   on the meaning of "peaceful coexistence,"
while the UN has been unable to define the word "aggression."
For some, "democracy" includes the authoritarian life,
   for others, "free world" embraces oppressive dictators.
In your Security Council
   can shouting between the nations replace sweet reason?
Or in your Southern cities
   can silence between the races resolve the conflict?
Your International Court is ineffective
   since the world cannot agree
   on the "principles of international law."
For Asians see this law as weighted toward colonialism,
   and Africans know it as rooted in racialism;
Latins agree its base is economic imperialism,
   Communists charge "capitalism" as its core.
Thus, mankind demands a universal speech,
and the name of that language is not Esperanto
   but Patience and Imagination and Love.

CHRISTIANITY—LEAVEN OR LUMP?

O my people of the law,
Would you make your Constitution conform to majority vote
   in every generation?

Or has it an eternal quality capable
    of guiding all generations?
Would you want the Koran read every morning in the public
        schools,
    or Moslem prayers forced on Protestant pupils?
Then why do you insist on the New Testament being read to
        Jews,
    or the Lord's Prayer recited by sons of agnostics?
Don't you understand that any prayer acceptable to the vast
        majority
    would, by its nature, be an affront to God—
    so broad as to be "weak tea" and "thin soup,"
a vain repetition
    like a bored conductor calling indistinguishable stops?
    How can we better train our youth to hate holy things?
Go back to your churches,
    and learn to be the leaven rather than the lump.

PRISONER OF POMPOSITY   (13:15-17)

Hear and give ear; be not proud,
    for the Lord has spoken.
Give glory to the Lord your God
    before he brings darkness.
Must you take every minor Communist achievement
    as a mortal blow?
Do you have to win every hand and every pot
    lest your dignity suffer without recover?
Are there no strategic retreats
    which herald final victory?
No quiet marches
    which raise the last battle's flag?
If you will not listen,
    my soul will weep in secret for your pride;
because pomposity has made you prisoner,
    and placed you in confinement so solitary
    your God is shut out.

GOD LOOKETH UPON THE HEART   (13:23)

Can the Ethiopian change his skin
or the leopard his spots?
How can you suddenly do good
when your heart is evil?
Can you instantly straighten out when your superior shows
his face?
The pupil folds his hands;
the clerk shuffles papers;
the factory worker looks busy;
the soldier stand erect;
the parishioner dusts off the Bible.
Do not be deceived;
God is not mocked.
His presence is constant.
He looks beneath the skin,
from the spots to the spotless,
to the center of your heart.

THE FAITHFUL SPIRITUAL LEADER   (14:13-15)

The prophets are prophesying lies in my name; I did not
send them, nor did I command them or speak to them. They
are prophesying to you a lying vision, worthless divination, and
the deceit of their own minds.
O unprofitable prophets! Your feet of clay
stand exposed beneath your flowing robes.
For you have been saying:
"What is needed most is peace of mind."
By gnawing ulcers, recurrent anxieties, and nervous
breakdowns
you prescribing prophets shall be incapacitated.
You have been saying, "Pray, have faith in faith,
and your afflictions will disappear."
By physical infirmities you shall be consumed,
infirmities not subject to cure by self-hypnosis.

You have been saying,
   "Think of yourself as a wealthy successful man.
   Focus the image in your mind.
   Carry it around with you and you will grow into it."
With a sense of failure unremoved by Pollyanna tricks
   you shall be obsessed.
You have been saying, "Don't be anxious.
   Surely the God who created the world
   would not permit it to be destroyed."
On that day you will have a box seat from which to view
   man's self-inflicted destruction,
   before you are utterly consumed.
Have you not heard of Tom Dooley, who, dying of cancer,
   used his medical instruments
   that he might be an instrument of God?
Do you not know of Albert Schweitzer,
   who, broken with nervous exhaustion,
   in the aftermath of World War I,
   returned to his beloved Lambarene,
   where healing others, he healed himself?
Is the name of Kagawa unfamiliar to you,
   that Japanese Christian, small of stature, big of heart,
   the "failure" who sat out the last war in prison,
   tarred and feathered for apologizing to the Chinese for
       his nation's aggression,
   one with the slum-dwellers of Kobe?
   Was his a Golden Boy success story?

So let the frustrated, ailing failures
   be the Kingdom of God at hand!
Not peace of mind,
   but a restless searching for God's will.
Not physical well-being, but spiritual growth.
Not the image of success, but the courage to risk failure.
Not praying for a *deus ex machina*,
   but compelling responsibility within the conscience of man.

BACKWARD PROGRESS   (15:5, 6)

Who will have pity on you, O America?
 Who will mourn your passing?
For *you have rejected me, says the Lord;*
 Your progress is all backward.
Thus, *I am weary of relenting.*
You have learned well the principles of mechanics,
 only to slaughter thousands on your highways.
You have stepped up the pace of your existence,
 leaving tranquilizers or mental illness the refuge of millions.
You have engaged your most brilliant scientists
 and applied their talents to works of destruction.
If you will not learn from your folly,
 what more can I do to correct you?
Must utter devastation come upon you,
 that your senses may be restored?

WARS REMEMBERED

I see an America that wants peace,
 but not enough,
because she has known war,
 but not enough,
not having suffered
 the bite of Russian winter,
 the firestorms of Dresden,
 the incessant bombings of London,
 the atomizing of Nagasaki.
When she remembers her most tragic war,
 she glorifies its anniversary
 with mock field battles.

LONELY TRUTH   (15:15-17)

Thy words were found, and I ate them,
 and thy words became to me a joy.
Yet *for thy sake I bear reproach,*

I did not sit in the company of merrymakers,
  nor did I rejoice;
for truth is a lonely hermit,
  and falsehood has many friends.

HOW THE WICKED PROSPER   (12:1-2; 17:10)

Why does the way of the wicked prosper?
  Why do all who are treacherous thrive?
Thou plantest them, and they take root;
  they grow and bring forth fruit;
thou art near in their mouth
  and far from their heart.
"I the Lord search the mind
  and try the heart,
to give to every man according to his ways,
  according to the fruit of his doings.
Do not be deceived by outward appearances.
Does the unscrupulous rich man have enough not to worry,
  or enough to cause him to worry?
Does the corrupt politician or labor leader
  believe that no one can touch him,
  or does he live in constant fear of assault?
Do the multiple marriages of many movie stars
  bring true happiness,
  or do they so cheapen a holy institution
  that it is converted to a worthless object?
Does the dishonest business man
  enjoy the accumulation of his wealth,
  or is he possessed with an unhappy obsession
  that it is not enough?
Now you see through a glass darkly,
  but then face to face.
Now you know in part,
  but then you shall know even as you are also known.

THE ARMS RACE   (21:8)

I set before you the way of life and the way of death.
    Therefore choose life.
Would you rather be dead than Red?
Do corpses march to the ballot box demanding their franchise?
    or slaughterers of the innocent stand guiltless before God?
Could you die with a smile upon your face,
    if, by annihilating 175 million non-Communist Russians,
    and countless fellow Americans,
    you could take Soviet leaders with you to the grave?
Would you rather be dead than Red?
    I'd rather be alive and free!
Accuse me, if you will, of appeasement,
    of serving the enemy unwittingly,
but I have your well-being at heart,
    an interest in your future—that there will be one!
The seers of your nation said of old:
    "To arms! To arms for your sure defense!"
    "Give me liberty, or give me death!"
    And they were right.
Your late President said to this generation:
    "In an ever-spiraling arms race, a nation's security
    may be shrinking even as its arms increase."
    And he was right.
Your scientists have stated for all to hear:
    Unless the arms race is halted,
    1000-megaton bombs will be built,
    which, if exploded 300 miles up,
    could sear all life in six Western states.
Your statesmen have prophesied for all to take cognizance:
    Unless there is a disarmament agreement,
    nuclear arms will be spread among many nations.
Today only four in the H-bomb club.
    Next year, six? In three years, a dozen?
Today Russia, tomorrow Israel,
    the day after that China or West Germany?

Your biologists are saying, if you will give heed:
    A full-scale nuclear attack on our nation
    could render all arable land unusable.
Do you not know the signs of the times—
    that at the Nevada atomic testing grounds,
    the only plant which flourishes abundantly
    is a robust weed called "Russian thistle"!
Is this all you can promise to inheritors of the earth?
What are you doing to the earth that is the Lord's?
To be sure, there are those among you who say:
    "But these weapons are not meant for use, only deterrence.
For if we are sufficiently well-armed,
    no nation would consider attacking."
They speak with some truth,
    for no nation in its right mind would risk retaliation,
    the assured consequence of initiating nuclear war.
But what about the nation "not in its right mind"?
How can you be sure that all nuclear powers
    will always act rationally?
Can you always depend upon those in the seats of power
    to demonstrate restraint?
In your own generation you have seen rise to power
    a megalomaniac Hitler in Germany,
    a paranoid Stalin in Russia.
And in your own country, a two-month retired Secretary of
    Defense
    jumped to his death from a hospital window.
What about the next generation:
    Would experience justify more faith in them?
Come out of your trance!
Stop mouthing the same old answers,
    though new problems baffle and terrify!

FAITH FOR THE NEW WORLD

Work for the new world, struggling to be born,
    offspring of the old which must suffer and die to
        make way for the new.

Do you know your own offspring?
   Will you admit paternity?
Where there was chaos, let there be order!
Where there was anarchy, law!
Where there was tyranny, freedom!
Where there was despair, hope!
Where there was animosity, goodwill!
Where there was tension, peace!
Must the new earth be an idle dream?
   Only to those who lack faith.
Every man has faith in something:
   in spiritual providence, or a pair of baby shoes
      dangling in the windshield;
   in what God can do for him, or what money can do for him;
   in a good physician, or home remedies;
   in a God-revealed religion, or some man-concocted
      philosophy.
In what shall we place our faith:
   in a U. N. Peace Force, or national armies?
   in working out our differences with other countries, or
      "going it alone"?
   in the extension of the free world, or military alliances
      with dictators?
   in granting newly emerging nations the right to be neutral,
      or writing them off as Communist-dominated?
   in trusting the Russians in a disarmament agreement, or
      trusting the Russians to show restraint in an arms race?
   in the Kingdom of God and his righteousness, or the king-
      doms of men and their wickedness?

THE FALSE PROPHETS   (23:13-40)

In the prophets of America I saw a disquieting thing.
   They preached "peace of mind"
   and flurried through another frantic week.
In the prophets of Europe I saw a troubling thing.
   They preached the Christian faith

and locked themselves in their studies for another half-
    fortnight.
Woe unto you preachers who "manicure the minor morals"
    while the hand of evil strangles your people
    with prejudice, crime, and war.
Woe unto you preachers who for a sermon begin with a joke,
    expand the Scripture lesson with dull repetition,
    and then, so as to close by noon,
    quickly conclude with an inoffensive generality.
Therefore, I am against the prophets,
    who steal their words from one another,
    who are proud of paste-pot sermons,
    who brag that they can preach "Fosdick's sermons better
        than Harry Emerson,"
    who bawl out, "The Bible says . . . ," and proceed to pro-
        claim their own ideas,
    who mislead my people through graphic description of "the
        furniture of heaven and the temperature of hell,"
    whose psycho-Scheherazade sermons enable their listeners
        only to hang on the cliff for one more week.
Therefore, I will surely lift you up,
    and cast you away from my presence.
I will bring upon you everlasting reproach
    and perpetual shame.

CONCERNING THE PEACE CORPS

Spin the earth on its axis,
bring forth that day long-awaited,
when your finest young people
    are not conscripted to police the world,
    or to squander their too-much leisure
    on one-armed bandits and two-armed harlots,
    on shacking up and cheap foreign wine.
I see a calendar with every day a red-letter day,
    a day in which to make glad.
Greatest resource of the nation,

in broken step your youth march forth
with enthusiasm undampened by elder wet-blankets,
imagination not yet cast into the organization-man mold,
energy unsapped by age's toll,
friendliness unrestrained by practical protocol,
idealism undaunted despite a thousand "can't be done's."
I see them moving like an army, but not an army,
these modern pioneers, fully equipped with shovel and book.
They go, not as conscripts, but as volunteers,
not to wound or imprison,
but to teach and heal;
not to lay waste or destroy,
but to irrigate and make grow;
not to impress "our way of life,"
but to help develop "their way of life";
not to lord it over with power and wealth,
but to live modestly in the midst, and to share in meekness.
I see youth who were without purpose, now purposeful;
who groaned about their future with foreboding,
now alive with anticipation;
formerly ingrown and pampered,
now whose pity has moved 5000 miles from self.

V | SECOND ISAIAH

Second Isaiah—His Times and Ours

Is the book of Isaiah one book or is it two or more books? Is it the work of one prophet or of many prophets? Most biblical scholars agree that chapters 40-66 of the book of Isaiah were written by an author (or authors) different from the eighth-century prophet Isaiah of Jerusalem. Not only do style, content, and theological ideas differ, but it is apparent that the last twenty-seven chapters belong to a much later historical period. Jerusalem had been destroyed. In 587 B.C., as a result of invasions by Nebuchadrezzar of Babylonia, the holy city and its temple were leveled. Some 4600 persons, including many of the most cultured and gifted, were deported to Babylon. There they remained in exile until their release in 539 B.C. after the conquest of Babylon by King Cyrus of Persia.

Cyrus gave the Babylonian god Marduk credit for his victory. He issued a decree soon after his triumph, freeing all captive peoples and permitting them to return to their homelands. Although the Jews had not fared badly in Babylon—enjoying freedom of assembly, opportunities to trade and to farm—still a number of them did return to Judah with the thought of rebuilding Jerusalem and its temple.

The usual date given for the writing of chapters 40-55 is about 540 B.C., a short time before the end of the captivity period. In this section the geographical references appear to be Babylonian while the remaining chapters of the book seem to point to a Jerusalem setting. The vividness of the author's description of the manufacture of Babylonian idols gives evidence of an eyewitness account (44:9-17). His references to Cyrus by name (44:28; 45:1) tend also to define the historical period.

WHO WAS SECOND ISAIAH?

While the author of the last twenty-seven chapters of Isaiah is not identified in the text itself, experts are in accord that chapters 40-55 were written long after the work of Isaiah of Jerusalem. There seems to be a natural division of chapters 40-55 from 56-66. The former is exilic in background and tone whereas the latter appears to be postexilic. Largely for this reason the majority of scholars believe that these two sections were written by separate authors. However, this writer is inclined to agree with a rather respectable minority (including C. C. Torrey, Louis Finkelstein, and James D. Smart) who claim that chapters 40-66 were written by a single author.

We call this nameless prophet Second Isaiah largely because his writings found a place on the unused part of a scroll containing the oracles of Isaiah of Jerusalem. He has submerged his personal identity in his writings to focus full attention on his task of calling the Hebrew people to serve a universal redemptive God of love. The prophet's exultant spirit shines through his poems, which brought hope and courage to the exiles in Babylon. The people were in despair because they felt their God had let them down; they were constantly tempted to shift their allegiance to the "successful gods" of their exilic environment. Into this situation Second Isaiah, the spiritual leader of the exiles, brought a buoyant message which strengthened their faith in the Holy One of Israel and gave them hope that they would soon return to the religious community of their homeland.

THE MAJOR TEACHINGS OF SECOND ISAIAH

There is no question but that Second Isaiah builds much of his message on ideas first presented by the eighth-century prophet of Jerusalem. For instance, he accepts First Isaiah's concept of God as the Holy One of Israel. However, certain other recurring themes demonstrate Second Isaiah's creative and independent thought:

God is Redeemer. In various passages the prophet proclaims "The Holy One of Israel is your Redeemer" (54:5).

God's redemption of his people is to be manifested partly in social terms: the return of the exiles to Palestine, the rebuilding of Jerusalem, the restoration of the holy city, and the conversion of the nations. The Redeemer also works in an inward and spiritual manner. "I am he who blots out your transgressions for my own sake, and I will not remember your sins" (43:25). In fact, he has swept away Israel's transgressions "like a cloud," and her sins "like mist" (44:22).

Thus, the Redeemer who forgave Israel's sin would lead his people out of exile and into the land that was their own, much as he led them through the wilderness years before under the leadership of Moses and his successors.

"Fear not, for I have redeemed you;
    I have called you by name, you are mine.
When you pass through the waters I will be with you;
    and through the rivers, they shall not overwhelm you;
when you walk through fire you shall not be burned,
    and the flame shall not consume you" (43:1-2).

For Second Isaiah, *there was one God and he was universal.* His sovereign power was manifest in Babylon as it was in Judah. "I am God, and there is no other; I am God and there is none like me" (46:9). This was an extremely bold assertion for the leader of a small and insignificant band of exiles to make in the land of Babylon, where the mighty Marduk was worshiped. He proclaimed that Israel might not be the most powerful people, but her God was the most powerful—in fact, he was the only God that existed!

Although King Cyrus of Persia might have thought he moved triumphantly under the banner of Marduk, actually, asserted Second Isaiah, he was being used by the Lord. Concerning Cyrus, the Lord was saying, "I gird you, though you do not know me" (45:5). Second Isaiah's concept, as reflected here, seems to have been somewhat different from First Isaiah's view of Assyria as "the rod of God's anger." The sixth-century prophet emphasizes God's universality in a more positive way—God would not use a foreign power as a direct means of punishing Israel, but rather, by his insistent Spirit, he would urge such a power to be an instrument of justice on behalf of the beloved Hebrew nation.

Yahweh is the only true God; he is unique and incomparable. Second Isaiah contrasts him with the man-made idols of Babylon which, in order to escape destruction during the coming fall of that city, will have to be loaded by hand and carried off on beasts. Such dead gods cannot be compared with the living Lord, who is not carried but himself carries the people of Israel through all their troubles.

Israel was God's own people. The Holy One of Israel has a special relationship with his people. He says to them, "You are mine" and "I have chosen you." He has chosen them because they have been particularly responsive. True, there have been times when he has been tempted to cast them off due to their disloyalty. But in the mainstream of their history they have rejoiced under his yoke. The Lord has not chosen them for special privilege or exemption from judgment. They have a special obligation and responsibility to serve Yahweh's worldwide purposes: "I have given you as a covenant to the people, a light to the nations" (42:6). Israel, then, had a missionary calling to establish justice among all peoples and to carry the message of God's salvation to the ends of the earth. When one considers that during the exile period and immediately following, the Jewish community had tended to turn in upon itself with greater emphasis upon the priestly functions and elaborate prescriptions concerning the Sabbath, then all the more remarkable is this calling to a universal role.

Second Isaiah stresses the role of *the suffering servant.* Some of the most inspiring passages of the Old Testament are found in the "servant songs" (42:1-4; 49:1-6; 50:4-9; 52:13—53:12). There has been much discussion among biblical experts as to the identity of the servant. Some have supposed him to be an individual, perhaps the prophet Jeremiah, or Nehemiah. Others have thought in terms of either the actual or an idealized Israel, or at least a faithful remnant within Israel.

The most logical conclusion appears to be that Second Isaiah is referring to the Hebrew nation. Evidence for this view is found in 49:3 where the Lord says: "You are my servant, Israel, in whom I will be glorified." When one moves beyond the servant poems to other passages of Second Isaiah, he finds many references to the servant as Israel, for instance, 41:8 and 44:1.

The prophet is calling his people not only to a redemptive

role within their own community, but, by becoming a servant of humanity, they are to bring salvation to all mankind. "It is too light a thing that you should be my servant to raise up the tribes of Jacob . . . I will give you as a light to the nations" (49:6).

How shall Israel "be exalted and lifted up" and "be very high" before the nations? Not by means of violence or oppression, but through undeserved suffering borne for the sake of others. We know that such a people must in the end divide "a portion with the great," that vicarious suffering possesses redemptive power which deserves to triumph.

But the prophet's call, though given nominal respect, fell largely upon unresponsive hearts. Neither the Hebrew nation nor a faithful remant accepted the responsibility described so graphically by the poet prophet. It was left to Jesus of Nazareth six centuries later so completely to identify himself with the suffering servant role that it is impossible for a Christian to read the passages without his Lord coming to mind. Thus the lofty ideal held up in the servant songs became concrete reality in the person of Jesus Christ, through whose ministry of service and suffering death mankind truly is redeemed.

SECOND ISAIAH'S MESSAGE FOR THE MODERN ERA

Of such breadth and depth are the teachings of this prophet of the exile that it is difficult to isolate the insights which are most significant for today. However, I would choose three emphases:

God is both one and universal, spanning space and time. "I am God, and there is no other." Although those of us in the Judaeo-Christian tradition accept the concept of God as found in our Holy Scriptures, this does not rule out the possibility that God may have revealed himself in some measure to other peoples. To say that God has revealed his nature in only one way at only one time is, to paraphrase J. B. Phillips' expression, "making our God too small."

The Christian may feel that the revelation of truth in the New Testament is a cascade of living water which floods the recesses of his soul. Other religious expressions may, for him, be meandering streams or torpid tributaries. Yet all streams do reach the bottom of the mountain, and bring refreshment to those who drink.

"The Lord is the everlasting God," wrote Second Isaiah. Neither space nor time can confine him. Sometimes Christians think of the biblical period as the "Golden Age of Religion" when God was operative in his universe in ways his Spirit cannot be manifested today. However, if God "inhabits eternity" and is the same, yesterday, today, and forever, then nothing which occurred spiritually in the period from the Hebrew times to the early Christian era could not also happen today. Otherwise, God's vitality and power are sapped. God's Spirit works through receptive human beings, and we may be sure that when God seems powerless, he has "looked for an opening" and found none.

"Heaven is my throne and the earth is my footstool; what is the house which you would build for me, and what is the place of my rest?" (66:1). Such a viewpoint cannot permit us to believe in a tight little god who looks down with favor only upon the worshipers in our sanctuary. Nor can we take refuge in a white god who would protect us against conscience-stirring kneel-ins by Negroes. Surely not if we have learned that God's house "shall be called a house of prayer for all peoples" (56:7).

Nor can we worship a tribal god who judges other nations by their actions but our own nation by our noble intentions which are expressed in such ideas as, "Our advance bases are purely defensive in purpose while theirs are clearly an aggressive threat to our security." Our God is too big for this. Both his judgment and his love go out to all the earth. As Dr. Lowell B. Hazzard has stated: "We can only truly understand what is going on in our times as we seek a God's eye view, a view which transcends nationalism."

A New Age is being heralded. The poet-prophet of the sixth century B.C. sang of the new society his people would build with God's help as they returned to Jerusalem. "For behold, I create new heavens and a new earth" (65:17). God was to play a creative role in the development of the new era.

Changes are occurring today at so fast a pace that the mind

can scarcely grasp the facts of change before they give way to further alteration.

Some fifty states with about one billion people have achieved their independence since the close of World War II. Most of these nations and peoples, located in Africa and Asia, will need help in developing political, economic, and social institutions to facilitate free, stable, and productive societies.

The population explosion cannot be ignored. At the time Christ walked the earth there were about one-quarter of a billion people on this planet. This number had doubled by A.D. 1650, finally reaching one billion about the middle of the nineteenth century. The population doubled again by 1940. It stands at some three billion people today and is expected to climb to more than six billion by the end of the present century![1]

The United Nations has undergone revolutionary changes. With the addition of Kenya and Zanzibar, there are now 113 members in the General Assembly, which began with 51 members in 1945. It is entirely possible that by 1970 125 countries may participate in this Parliament of Man. Not only has the size of the General Assembly increased but also its authority. When the action by the veto-impaired Security Council was blocked, the General Assembly, operating under the "Uniting for Peace" resolution, took on new responsibility and prestige. How the smaller nations, who are now the majority in the UN, behave and demonstrate their maturity will largely determine the future role the UN will assume in keeping the peace.

The Western European nations, through their Common Market and European Free Trade Association, have become the largest group of exporters in the world. This recovery from post-war prostration, with the help of our Marshall Plan but also largely due to their own initiative and ingenuity, is one of the most amazing phenomena of the modern era. Whether the countries of the European Economic Community will now relate themselves with the United Kingdom and the United States in an enlarged trading community only the future will reveal.

Important changes have taken place in Eastern Europe which

have significance for the cause of freedom. In Poland, for instance, the press is now relatively free, able to criticize its own government without fear of reprisal. Both Poland and Yugoslavia have free access to Western books, magazines, films, and unjammed Voice of America broadcasts. Under our economic aid program a thousand Yugoslav students have spent a year in this country to gain technical knowledge, and they were incidentally exposed to our free institutions. The position taken by Yugoslavia in the United Nations has more often been an independent one, free of automatic agreement with the Communist bloc. Today, surprisingly enough, Hungarians enjoy more freedom than any other people in Eastern Europe with the possible exception of Poland. Consequently the seventeenth session of the General Assembly accepted the credentials of the present Hungarian government and they are now seated in the United Nations.

In the United States a veritable revolution is taking place in race relations. Under the impact of the non-violent direct action movement, public accomodations are opening up to all people. With the passage of the Civil Rights Bill of 1964 further progress toward an inclusive society is being and will be made, for we can be sure that the Negro community is not going to wait forever to enjoy the fruits of liberty which they consider their due as American citizens. As one Negro leader phrased it: "We have waited for more than three hundred and forty years for our constitutional and God-given rights. The nations of Asia and Africa are moving with jet-like speed toward a goal of political independence, and we still creep at horse and buggy pace toward the gaining of a cup of coffee at a lunch counter."[2]

In the unfolding New Age, spiritual resources and moral guidance will be indispensable. The Christian sees his task much as Second Isaiah saw his: "Prepare the way of the LORD, make straight . . . a highway for our God" (40:3). We must seek to open channels so that God's Spirit can operate effectively in a swiftly changing society.

We are called to fulfill the role of the suffering servant. How is the New Age to be implemented? Not, said the sixth-century prophet, with the instruments of violence and bloodshed, of power and oppression. Rather, he called his people as a corporate community to adopt for themselves the role of suffering and sacrificial service on behalf of others.

Twenty centuries ago Christ assumed this role on behalf of all humanity. Following his example, spiritually motivated individuals and small groups have taken up the task, but the prophet's call still beckons all those who would usher in the New Age.

Is the Christian church responding to the call through its worldwide missionary enterprise? The average Christian who gives only a few dollars a year for the cause of missions can hardly qualify as a "sacrificial servant" of humanity. Yet the church has demonstrated its capacity to serve compassionately in time of great need: assisting refugees in Algeria, Hong Kong, and Taiwan; resettling escapees from Hungary and Cuba.

Another group which has taken on the burdens of the suffering servant has been the Negro people of the United States, or at least a sizeable minority among these 20 million Americans. They have sought the redemptive way, through nonviolence and suffering love, to win civil rights and human dignity. Like the ancient Hebrews in Babylon, American Negroes yearn for freedom. As the Jewish community enjoyed some privileges during their life in exile, so the Negro has been granted some privileges in American society. Now he is asking for his full rights.

Through economic aid to developing nations, the United States has borne some of the sorrows of less privileged peoples. An American society which enjoys a per capita income of $2500 a year feels itself under substantial obligation in a world where the per capita income in many nations is less than $50 a year. We are spending more than two billion dollars around the world for such projects as building dams, providing irrigation, drilling wells, sharing agricultural techniques, training teachers, controlling and curing disease, and promoting sanitation. Nevertheless, our total aid program including the Alliance for Progress in Latin America costs the United States less than one-half of the amount which has been suggested as a reasonable goal: one per cent of our Gross National Product.

If our purposes are misunderstood and we are the victims of ingratitude, "despised and rejected," this should be expected by a great power and ought not to discourage us from doing what needs to be done.

Perhaps the most significant government effort through which American citizens are seeking to serve humanity directly and at some personal sacrifice is the Peace Corps program. These 7000 volunteers, mostly young people, have gone out to serve in 44 countries in Africa, Latin America, the Far East, the Near East, and South Asia. They are helping to build roads into inaccessible areas which previously had no markets available for their agricultural produce. They are demonstrating culture of fruit trees, giving penicillin shots, and showing villagers how to build sturdier homes of mud brick.

Poverty, ignorance, and disease, hatred, fear, and prejudice, still weigh heavily upon millions of God's children. Only as the strong voluntarily share the burdens of the weak and the consequences of human insensitivity can the vision of the new heaven and the new earth be fulfilled.

Selections from Second Isaiah

THE ONENESS OF GOD   43:10-12

"You are my witness," says the LORD,
   "and my servant whom I have chosen,
that you may know and believe me
   and understand that I am He.
Before me no god was formed,
   nor shall there be any after me.
I, I am the LORD,
   and besides me there is no savior.
I declared and saved and proclaimed,
   when there was no strange god among you;
   and you are my witnesses," says the LORD.

SUFFERING SERVANT OF THE LORD   53:2-7, 12

He had no form or comeliness that we should look at him,
   and no beauty that we should desire him.
He was despised and rejected by men;
   a man of sorrows, and acquainted with grief;
and as one from whom men hide their faces
   he was despised, and we esteemed him not.
Surely he has borne our griefs
   and carried our sorrows;
yet we esteemed him stricken,
   smitten by God, and afflicted.
But he was wounded for our transgressions,
   he was bruised for our iniquities;
upon him was the chastisement that made us whole;
   and with his stripes we are healed.
All we like sheep have gone astray;
   we have turned every one to his own way;
and the LORD has laid on him
   the iniquity of us all.

He was oppressed, and he was afflicted,
  yet he opened not his mouth;
like a lamb that is led to the slaughter,
  and like a sheep that before its shearers is dumb,
  so he opened not his mouth.
. . .he poured out his soul to death,
  and was numbered with the transgressors;
yet he bore the sin of many,
  and made intercession for the transgressors.

RETURN TO THE LORD   55:6-8

Seek the LORD while he may be found,
  call upon him while he is near;
let the wicked forsake his way,
  and the unrighteous man his thoughts;
let him return to the LORD, that he may have mercy on him,
  and to our God, for he will abundantly pardon.
For my thoughts are not your thoughts,
  neither are your ways my ways, says the LORD.

SIN SEPARATES YOU FROM GOD   59:1-4, 7-8

Behold, the LORD's hand is not shortened, that it cannot save,
  or his ear dull, that it cannot hear;
but your iniquities have made a separation
  between you and your God,
and your sins have hid his face from you
  so that he does not hear.
For your hands are defiled with blood
  and your fingers with iniquity;
your lips have spoken lies,
  your tongue mutters wickedness.
No one enters suit justly,
  no one goes to law honestly;
they rely on empty pleas, they speak lies,
  they conceive mischief and bring forth iniquity. . . .
Their feet run to evil,
  and they make haste to shed innocent blood;

their thoughts are thoughts of iniquity,
  desolation and destruction are in their highways.
The way of peace they know not,
  and there is no justice in their paths;
they have made their roads crooked,
  no one who goes in them knows peace.

A LIGHT FOR THE NATIONS 60:1-3

Arise, shine; for your light has come,
  and the glory of the LORD has risen upon you.
For behold, darkness shall cover the earth,
  and thick darkness the peoples;
but the LORD will arise upon you,
  and his glory will be seen upon you.
And nations shall come to your light,
  and kings to the brightness of your rising.

CREATION OF A NEW JERUSALEM 65:17-20, 21-25

For behold, I create new heavens
  and a new earth;
and the former things shall not be remembered
  or come into mind.
But be glad and rejoice for ever
  in that which I create;
for behold, I create Jerusalem a rejoicing,
  and her people a joy.
I will rejoice in Jerusalem,
  and be glad in my people;
no more shall be heard in it the sound of weeping
  and the cry of distress.
No more shall there be in it
  an infant that lives but a few days,
  or an old man who does not fill out his days . . .
They shall build houses and inhabit them;
  they shall plant vineyards and eat their fruit.
They shall not build and another inhabit;
  they shall not plant and another eat;

for like the days of a tree shall the days of my people be,
  and my chosen shall long enjoy the work of their hands.
They shall not labor in vain,
  or bear children for calamity;
for they shall be the offspring of the blessed of the LORD,
  and their children with them.
Before they call I will answer,
  while they are yet speaking I will hear.
The wolf and the lamb shall feed together,
  the lion shall eat straw like the ox;
  and dust shall be the serpent's food.
They shall not hurt or destroy
  in all my holy mountain,

                                        says the LORD.

Second Isaiah—A Universal Spirit for an Age of Peace

THE UNIVERSAL GOD* (43:10)

Before me no god was formed,
nor shall there be any after me.
Is there a God of the Moslem?
Is there a God of the Buddhist?
Is there a God of the Hindu?
Is there a God of the Christian?
Nay, for I am God, and there is no other.
I am the first and the last
and all that lies between.
I am the only God men have ever known.
I was the same at the first as I shall be at the last.
When men pray, it is to me they lift their voices.
Their prayers may be private,
but I am a public God.
I have never had a chosen people
except those who chose to serve me.
No man has been elected,
except as he has elected to be used for my purposes.
Prayers have come for rain in drought,
for victory, and defeat of enemies,
for length of life, for the mercy of death.
The Judge of the universe hears them all.
I am the Sun God, the Moon God, the God of the Gentle Rain,
the God of Fertility, and of those in mobility;
I am the God of Moses and Jesus, of Augustine and Luther.

---

* In this paraphrase I do not intend to discount Divine Initiative, but rather I think of it as a given—capable of working through any peoples or person willing to respond. Without response, neither the Hebrews nor Christ could have become *chosen servants.*

I am the God with whom all men must come to terms, late or
    soon.
True, some have fashioned me in the image of their ultimates.
They have made wealth their god
    and have been laid purseless in the casket.
They have made power their life principle
    and have lived to a feeble old age.
They have made personality development their idol
    and the mortician has hired their pallbearers.
Moslems walk barefoot into my mosques.
Jews elevate the Torah in my temples.
Catholics take Holy Communion in my sanctuaries.
Protestants sing joyful hymns in my churches.
They are all my people,
    and those who choose me are my chosen people.

THE SUFFERING SERVANT   (52:14—53:12)

His appearance was so marred,
    beyond human semblance.
Is it a man?
    His blood flows red,
    his tears are salty,
    his sweat runs down.
He had no form or comeliness
    that we should look at him.
    His nose was too broad,
    lips too thick,
    hair too curly.
And no beauty that we should desire him.
    Would you want your daughter to marry one?
He was despised and rejected by men.
    He knew a door, not as an entranceway,
        but as a barrier to be shut in one's face:
        "Exclusive subdivision";
        "Private swimming club";
        "We reserve the right to choose our guests";
        "Opportunities for ambitious junior executives."

A man of sorrows,
  he sang comforting spirituals,
  finding his solace in an understanding God
  who alone knew the trouble he'd seen.
Acquainted with grief,
  he could be shot for a quarter,
  and his mourners would see
    a white jury grant his murderer a hunting license.
Yet we esteemed him stricken,
  smitten by God, and afflicted:
  "curse of Noah"—"sons of Ham";
  "white and black"—"good and evil";
  "pure Aryan stock"—"mongrelized Negroid";
  "marked by the Almighty" — "white man's burden."
But he was wounded for our transgressions,
  he was bruised for our iniquities.
  The white man brought him here,
    put him in chains and beat him.
  When he was given liberty,
    and sought to rise a free man,
    he was beaten down again to keep him in his place.
Upon him was the chastisement that made us whole,
  and with his stripes we are healed.
  As he strode uncowed to freedom,
    our sense of human dignity deepened.
  As his flesh was torn open,
    the bleeding sore of our bitterness healed.
  We are healed of our inheritance
    of ingrained prejudice.
  We are healed of our pride
    in an innate superiority.
  We are healed of our separateness
    that fragments the human species,
  knowing now no whiteness of skin is purer
    than suffering love.
We have turned every one to his own way.
  "It's none of my business."

"Why be subject to economic reprisals?"
"A problem of time and education;
  can't do anything about it now."
Like a sheep that before its shearers is dumb,
  so he opened not his mouth.
  They sat at the lunch counter, quiet and contained,
    unresponsive to taunts or jeers of the crowd.
  In a reverent silence that spoke of proudest grief,
    thousands marched behind the bier of their slain leader.
He poured out his soul to death.
  "Scattered shots through curtained windows";
  "Homemade bomb ripped bedroom wall";
  "Murdered in the driveway";
    but they never cut him down.
He *was numbered with the transgressors,*
  set upon by dogs trained for catching thieves,
  prodded by charged goading sticks designed to herd cattle,
  struck by violent streams of water.
    "Can't put out the fire!"
Yet he bore the sin of many,
  twenty per cent without Caucasian blood.
    "Separate but equal" equals unequal.
    "The last to be hired, and the first fired."
    "The right to live next door—to somebody else."
They gathered in the house of God
and made intercession for the transgressors,
  lifting prayers with hearts and voices,
  hearts fervent, voices shrill,
  "Ku Klux Klan," "Citizens Council,"
  "Do not lay their sins against
    who by our struggle are incensed."

THE AGE OF PEACE   (55:3-12; 49:6, 17; 55:12; 65:21-25)

Thus says the Lord:
  Incline your ear and come to me;
    hear, that your soul may live;

and I will make with you an everlasting covenant,
  my steadfast, sure love for my people...
For as the heavens are higher than the earth,
  so are my ways higher than your ways
  and my thoughts than your thoughts...
For as the rain and the snow come down from heaven,
  and return not thither but water the earth,
making it bring forth and sprout,
  giving seed to the sower and bread to the eater,
so shall my word be that goes forth from my mouth;
  it shall not return to me empty,
but it shall accomplish that which I purpose,
  and prosper in the thing for which I sent it.
For you shall go out in joy,
  and be led forth in peace.
In that day the flowering dogwood shall stretch out its limbs,
  as a many-armed waiter carrying a dozen bouquets as trays;
and the crepe myrtle shall send forth its blooms,
  like circus candy on a stick;
and the weeping willow will arch her branches to the water's
      edge,
  like a woman washing her long green hair in a flowing
      stream.
And all shall dwell in a land of beauty,
  praising God for his wondrous gifts to the children of men,
For a new age shall dawn,
  and it shall not be called the Space Age,
  or the Jet Age or the Atomic Age,
  but the Age of Peace:
an age when men will beat their tanks into tractors,
  their rockets into mail-service missiles,
  their atom bombs into power plants.
For this will be an age
  when *your builders* will *outstrip your destroyers,*
where resources, once used for arms soon obsolete,
  will pour into schools and cathedrals of healing,
    into teachers' salaries and urgent medical research;

where talents wasted on war strategy
   are redirected to the strategy of peace;
where young Americans are not sent out to police the world
      with force,
   but to serve the world with talent and friendship,
not to train guerrillas or anti-guerrillas,
   but to train teachers and farmers.
For *I will give you as a light to the nations,*
   that my salvation may reach to the end of the earth.
Let the trumpets proclaim
   that a generation has come of age!
Let the mountains and hills *break forth in singing*
   and all the trees of the field clap their hands!
For the spell of war-obsession has been broken,
   and the paranoid world has regained her senses.
The promise of a new era
   hangs like ripe fruit on a bowed-down tree;
a time when man may travel freely in any portion of the world,
   his humanity his passport;
when broadcasts are unjammed
   and so are roads;
when nations are not inclined to hide their bombs,
   but anxious to share their vaccines;
when scientists may freely trade their information and
      discoveries,
   and no government will circumscribe truth with political
      theory.
Let that age step forth with eagerness
   as a bridegroom cometh from his chamber;
when every man may speak his mind
   with no knock on the door at midnight;
when religion may be taught to all who desire its benefits;
   when no press release suffers prior censorship,
      nor any peaceful assembly is disturbed by police;
   when rich nations share compassionately with poor,
      not out of fear, or threat, or contest;

when no land will be a law unto itself,
   but all accept a common rule of justice;
when men are not joined only to their likeness, exclaiming:
   "He's a Mason!" or "He's a Catholic!"
   "He's a Negro!" or "He's a Caucasian!"
   "He's a Christian!" or "He's a Communist!"
   "He's an American!" or "He's a Russian!"
but rather shall they rejoice
   in the unity that makes them brothers,
   proclaiming: "He's my fellowman!"
That winsome new age shall awake
   when all men *enjoy the work of their hands.*
They shall build houses and inhabit them;
   they shall plant vineyards and eat their fruit.
They shall not build and another inhabit;
   they shall not plant and another eat . . .
They shall not labor in vain
   or bear children for calamity . . .
Before they call I will answer,
   while they are yet speaking I will hear.
The wolf and the lamb shall feed together,
   the lion shall eat straw like the ox . . .
They shall not hurt or destroy
   in all my holy mountain,

                                   says the Lord.

NOTES AND ACKNOWLEDGMENTS

Chapter I, Amos

1. Reinhold Niebuhr, "A Critique of Pacifism," *Atlantic Monthly*, Vol. 139 (May 1927), p. 639.
2. *Accident Facts* (Chicago: National Safety Council, 1961), p. 48.
3. Roger Ragan, "Methodists and Residential Segregation of the Negro," *Concern* (July 15, 1963), pp. 4-5.

Chapter II, First Isaiah

1. G. G. D. Kilpatrick, "Isaiah," in *The Interpreter's Bible,* Vol. V (New York: Abingdon Press, 1956), p. 333.
2. S. Paul Schilling, *Isaiah Speaks* (New York: Woman's Division of Christian Service, Board of Missions of The Methodist Church, 1958), p. 62.
3. Seymour Melman, ed., *A Strategy for American Security* (New York: Lee Service, Inc., 1963), p. 1.

Chapter III, Jonah

1. Edna St. Vincent Millay, "Renascence," in *Renascence and Other Poems* (New York: Harper & Brothers, 1940).

Chapter IV, Jeremiah

1. Paul Tillich elaborates helpfully on this idea in his book *The New Being* (New York: Charles Scribner's Sons, 1955), pp. 9 ff.
2. Melman, *op. cit.*, pp. 1-2.
3. John J. McCloy, "Why the World Will Disarm," *This Week Magazine* (Dec. 10, 1961).

Chapter V, Second Isaiah

1. Haskell Miller and Dale White, *Meeting the Needs of the World's People* (Washington: Board of Christian Social Concerns of The Methodist Church, 1962), p. 4.
2. Martin Luther King, Jr., "Letter From Birmingham City Jail" (Philadelphia: American Friends Service Committee, 1963), p. 5.

SELECTED BIBLIOGRAPHY

Buttrick, George A., ed., *The Interpreter's Bible* (especially Vols. 5 and 6). New York: Abingdon Press, 1956.

Case, Harold C., *The Prophet Jeremiah*. New York: Woman's Division of Christian Service, Board of Missions of The Methodist Church, 1953.

Chase, Mary Ellen, *The Prophets for the Common Reader*. New York: W. W. Norton & Company, Inc., 1963.

Hamilton, Edith, *Spokesmen for God*. New York: W. W. Norton and Company, Inc., 1949.

Heaton, E. W., *The Old Testament Prophets*. Baltimore, Md.: Penguin Books, Inc., 1958.

Heschel, Abraham J., *The Prophets*. New York: Harper and Row, 1962.

Kelly, Balmer H., ed., *The Layman's Bible Commentary*, Vol. 11, *Isaiah*, by G. Ernest Wright; Vol. 12, *Jeremiah, Lamentations*, by Howard T. Kuist; Vol. 14, *Hosea, Joel, Amos, Obadiah, Jonah*, by Jacob M. Myers. Richmond, Va.: John Knox Press, 1964, 1959, 1960.

Leslie, Elmer A., *Isaiah*. New York: Abingdon Press, 1963.

Leslie, Elmer A., *Jeremiah*. New York: Abingdon Press, 1954.

Leslie, Elmer A., *The Prophets Tell Their Own Story*. New York: Abingdon Press, 1939.

Phillips, J. B., *Four Prophets*. New York: The Macmillan Company, 1963.

Schilling, S. Paul, *Isaiah Speaks*. New York: Woman's Division of Christian Service, Board of Missions of The Methodist Church, 1958.

Scott, R. B. Y., *The Relevance of the Prophets*. New York: The Macmillan Company, 1944.

Smart, James D., *Servants of the Word*. Philadelphia: The Westminster Press, 1960.

Smith, J. M. P., *The Prophets and Their Times*, 2nd ed. rev. by William A. Irwin. Chicago: University of Chicago Press, 1941.

NCMC BS 1505.7 .C67 1965
Corbett, J. Elliott 1920-
The prophets on Main Street

DATE DUE

12/22/12